glenn's proof copy

Still s
for t
Big City Beats

by

Glenn Carmichael & Evan Evans

Published by:

PIMP$ of the ALPHAB£T PRESS

130c Lower Cheltenham Place
Montpelier
Bristol BS6 5LF

British Library Cataloguing in Publication Data.
A catalogue record for this book is available from the British Library.

First Edition
Published 2000

ISBN: 0-9526432-5-1

Cover photo by Nick Constance
Proofing by Sara-Jane Arbury
Design & Layout by Glenn Carmichael
Cover notes by Jon Andriessen

Printed & bound in Ireland by:
Colour Books Ltd.
Unit 105 Baldoyle Industrial Estate, Baldoyle, Dublin 13.

All characters and situations portrayed in this novel are fictitious.

What kind of journey is the life of a human being that it has a beginning but not an end?

Jack Kerouac

One

I've been searching, I've been looking, for something, one thing that's tangible, something I can hold on to, the recognisable piece that'll make sense of this crazed hotchpotch of a jigsaw, a definite thread that'll unravel this tangled tapestry of my memory. Something that pulls all the loose ends; snapping strings of questions, that whip us like a slave driver on a Roman galley ship. Yeah, exactly like those old beat down slaves, straining on their oars, to the thud of the drum, part of them still hanging on to a dream of freedom, hoping there's still a chance if they make port alive, another part so despairing, they hope the whole ship goes down, and then there would be an end to their suffering, their misery.... I'm looking for something more than hope. I'm looking for something real, something palpable. I'm on a mission. I'm on a trip. I'm taking in too much memory. There's nothing definite about memory. There's only one thing that's certain....

"Yip, yip, yippa ya eh," Gene yodels, with a loud slap to my shoulder, cracking me out of my reverie. "Look at that! Just look at that building! Awesome! Such an impressive edifice. The Embankment gives me a hard-on. I know I'm in London when I'm hitting the Embankment's black top. Just look at those lights! South Bank sodium soporific sentinel, keep watching over the Big Smoke. Big Brother, we know you are watching over us. We who are about to die salute you. Look, look can't you see? Cleopatra's Needle, Rome's Golden Eagle. *Et tu* Brutus. Spikey baby? Brother!..."

"Just keep your hands on the wheel, and your eyes on the road," I snap, "or we may be meeting our maker earlier than expected."

Gene has a habit of forgetting that we're mere mortals, and cars are fast moving steel machines, capable of horrible injury to flabby flesh, causing serious damage and untimely death. I suppose this may be the difference between passengers and drivers, the difference between me and G. Being a pavement pounder myself, I have a healthy respect for the wheels of steel. White lines - don't cross that zebra crossing. Is this pedestrian paranoia? Gene has some other kind of view about crossing the line - some other paranoia - white line fever - don't do it!

Gene laughs, and shouts, "Lighten-up; this is one hell of a journey - the Beats go West to kick some ass. *Young man there's no need to be down...* Earls Court, here we come! Keeping the flame of poetry burning. Yeah, burn baby burn. *Come on baby light my fire.*"

The G is flying high as usual. Got to get his feet back on the ground. It isn't funny, considering my respect for my own mortality and motor cars, that I am in this hell on wheels with the G man. I don't think too much about the consequences, or about how any drivers I share a car with are going to cope with the results of their actions at the wheel; it's their responsibility. Am I irresponsible? Maybe. But these days with the big A killing all before it, and retrospectively too, I guess it would be too much to ask drivers to fill in a questionnaire about their attitudes to speed limits. There's probably more worries about who you're sharing your bed with, than thinking about your travelling companion's concerns of careering at speed down highways with complete strangers. It fits, considering more people die in their own beds than in their cars... or other people's cars.

I say firmly to Gene, "Let's make sure we get there in one piece, or there won't be any kicking ass but our own."

It's a message that gets no reaction but another pull on the joint that is a constant companion for the G. Now I am not a moralist, or in any way wish to be judge and jury on the drug issue. Hell I toke the odd spliff now and then. My problem is it's always someone else's spliff. I'm just no good at rolling my own, and as I don't smoke cigarettes, soft drugs are strictly an area I don't get involved in. G is more erudite and articulate than most, and despite his massive consumption of the herb, he always appears to be on an even keel; a little crazy, but then whose sane after Hiroshima?

Gene rolls his eyes, smokes his joint and yells at the top of his voice, "Beats, Beats, Beats, Beats... Big City Beats!" passes me his spliff and remarks, "You take life too seriously. As Jim said, no one gets out of here alive, but it's up to us to jump and jive."

"*I want to take you on a journey into sound. Stereophonic sound - - Stereophonic sound. This is a trip. This is a trip.*" G's intently singing along with the stereo.

Times like this - just me and the G, was real. All my days at the office, pushing paper and answering the telephone - all my time with my partner, watching television, cooking, washing, shopping - all of this was like background static in my life, compared to the bright images left in my mind of the time spent, just me and the G.

"Ladies and gentlemen, I have great pleasure in introducing you to London's foremost gurus of the spoken word. The most brilliant performance poetry duo ever.... The BIG CITY BEATS! **Ye-e-eh,**

Yeh, Yeh!"

"Oops!!" Gene swings the wheel, narrowly missing colliding with another car as he drifts into the middle lane.

"Fuck!" I say.

"Sorry Spike! I'm sorry."

Silence ensues.

I'm a passenger in somebody else's transport - I'm always the passenger. Life passes by, through glass, as I gaze at the city, in silence - a silent protest - round Parliament Square, down Great George Street, Horse Guards Road, and into The Mall. It doesn't take long for G to move back into the spotlight, after his brief, silent sojourn on the sidelines. He strikes up another spliff, inserts another cassette...

"Well I'm up on the 11th floor, and I'm watching the cruisers below." It's David Bowie's 'Queen Bitch'.

Looking back I wonder just how much was real to Gene. He was constantly doing his best to make life a big play; pull the strings on his own reality. If the world was a movie set, and he was lead actor and director, what part was I playing? Or was I just a member of the audience; the passenger?

The roundabout outside Buckingham Palace, and Gene's bobbing about in his seat.

"She's a queen, and such a Queen, and such an actor..."

Bang! We hit the tail of another car, trying to turn into Constitution Hill. Gene stops, swings open the door, saying, "Spike, roll down your window." He's in the road, dodging traffic, and running over towards the car he's dented. There's a policeman rocking on his heels outside the Palace, looking incredibly ill at ease... I wind down the window, and sit and watch, as the movie moves into quick edit - and the director.... directs.

He's apologising profusely to some shocked woman, he's fussing around looking overtly concerned for her welfare, her car; maybe my perception wasn't too sharp, but I'd swear he was flirting; he's got her by the elbow and gently guides her back to her seat; he's closed her door, and is squatting down, elbows on the sill, whispering a last few condolences, then he's spinning round and up, with an almost imperceptible wave over his shoulder. How does he do it? I've had a couple of tokes on his spliffs, and my head's gone - I'm sat here in a damaged motor, in the middle of the road, directly outside Buckingham Palace with a jittery policeman full of fresh paranoia, after the Queen's had a gun pulled on her during the trooping of the colour, a maniac sitting on her bed, and the IRA have raised their campaign of bombing the mainland... and G's in his element. Thank God I'm only a bit player in this psycho drama, I couldn't handle a main part in such an intense scene, but then I haven't had the rehearsals Gene's had. The movies he makes are never boring.

Gene's coming in my direction, but he doesn't look at me - he's looking straight ahead, looking straight at the policeman - he's smiling, a warm and open smile. He turns his palms upwards and shrugs his shoulders - an obvious and deferentially expressive gesture, as if saying, "Look, sorry - shit happens!" The policeman is talking into his radio. Fuck knows what he's thinking.

Gene looks cool, very cool, completely in black, with his two piece suit, roll neck and thick-soled loafers, short cropped hair. He walks with relaxed confidence, but I notice without the usual swagger. He's right next to the policeman, slightly to one side, so the bobby can keep an eye on the road, on the car, on me. G's expressively motioning with his hands; broad, free and easy sweeps of his arms. He's handing the policeman something, he pats him on the shoulder. He turns towards the car; still no register of my existence. He's anticipating the mad hubbub of traffic. He passes in front of the car, I watch through the windscreen - through glass. This is like some new form of television, where the viewer feels involved in the drama on screen - involved, but not involved, always through glass, always at a distance. Gene has stopped on the off side, fists on his hips, head cocked on one side. He bends down, he's out of my sight, 'off screen', he's pulling at the wheel arch or somewhere - I just sit and watch - it's not my car - I know nothing about cars.

I'm sat watching, I can just see the top of his head and his shoulders straining. He's stood back up, he's looking at me, he gives a gesture with his hands as if saying, "That's the best I can do!" - his gestures are at me, but not for me - he gestures as an actor would gesture - for the audience. And then he's opening the door, swinging inside, back in the driving seat.

"Spike," he exclaims, "you could have got rid of the roach!"

I can't say anything.

He reaches under his seat, pulls out a brown envelope, shoves it down the front of his trousers, "Let's get the fuck out of here before the S.P.G. arrive!"

"What happened? What did you say?" I ask, as we move along Constitution Hill towards Hyde

Park Corner.

"Well, her name's Irene, and she's terribly worried, cos this is the second bump she's had this month, and her husband was so angry last time. I told her not to worry, I'd take full responsibility. She was quite cute - I felt quite horny - I've got her number - she could probably do with an affair; her husband sounds like a pig."

"Yeah, but the *policeman...?*"

"Oh, he didn't really seem to wanna get involved, I think he's got other stuff on his plate right now. Anyway, I appealed to his male chauvinism and he agreed that all women are terrible motorists. I gave him my card."

"Fuck!!" I say.

Gene begins to laugh. "We'd better get a move on Spikey-babe, we're late for work. Beats, Beats, Bea-a-ts!"

The two of us are on the road, with no Kerouac to guide us, no Ginsberg to howl, no Hunter S Thompson to interpret the fear and loathing. The G-man is doing a bloody good imitation of all three. He's just inserted another cassette, rapping along with our mentors The Last Poets, *"Cos the white man's got a God complex..."*

Round Hyde Park Corner and down Knightsbridge, I become very aware of the boundaries that divide East from West – it's a money boundary. I'm musing on the difference to our main drag in E1; the Whitechapel strip... and suddenly I realise, this is not the route we'd normally drive to Earls Court. "Gene, why are we coming this way?"

"Oh, didn't I say? I've just got to drop in to see someone on the way, it won't take a minute... It's just here."

He's pulling in to the forecourt of The

Carlton, he turns and smiles, and says, "Just relax Spike, I'll be seconds."

He's out of the car and through the main doors. I sit with the soundtrack declaring, *"I got Jones comin' down."* I know this has got to be a drug connection. Everyone has to make a living. We never talk about it - it's one of two things we never talked about.

I do not like sitting outside The Carlton Hotel in Knightsbridge in a damaged Vauxhall Victor, while the G is doing God knows what, with God knows who, and The Last Poets are declaring *"Niggers are afraid of revolution"*, but it's not my car, it's not my drug deal. I switch off the cassette and sit in the passenger seat and wait - the passenger. I close my eyes so I'm not really here. I try and sum up some indignation, something I can say to make Gene apologise for his behaviour, but as ever I know there's nothing to say. I know I'm here by choice - nobody made me get involved.

Gene and me had a history. We had been small time successes fronting a leather-clad rap band, The White Brothers. We advertised ourselves as 'London's première rappers'. We were almost famous. We believed the only reason we didn't become huge stars was cos we were before our time (that's what we told each other!). One day I'd rung Gene up moaning about how much I missed those days.

He'd said "Let's be poets!"

I said "O.K."

At the time neither of us knew anything about the poetry world; but we soon found out. We trod round London's dead-bed poetry societies, we checked out 'the scene' - hell there was no scene, just a disparate, desperate collection of individuals who had one common thread: poetry. Their words sad, funny, mostly confused; stumbling around like lost children, lost voices, hoping for a smattering of applause, or to suckle the milk of human kindness. Zombies in Limbo's waiting-room, gathering together to try to find some kind of comfort - waiting... Waiting for something. Waiting in basements, rooms above pubs. Displaying their hand-crafted wares to like-minded individuals, who had too much of the same kind of commodity - nobody was buying. Lost souls reaching out, and hoping, that every once in a while their words might touch something, or somebody. A motley crew; the proverbial mixed bag - take your pick. Ages, sexes, race, varied, but predominately elderly and male. If I could draw an analogy, poetry in the late 80's was like a cosy, smoky, gentleman's club, where old fuckers exchange terse nods over newspapers. But nobody gets too close. Silence is the mode. When you're in an exclusive club, you get smug, the clientele feel safe with the familiarity, the tradition, the furniture; ensconced in their comfortable niche; content and conceited. Armchairs, pipes and slippers have been passed around, and the dust of time settles down, as the world grinds around and everyone snoozes.

Suddenly the car door opens, "Hey Spike we ain't got time for cat napping, lets go cruise The Court."

So it's back to the road, the journey, the mission; the bards of E1 go West.

"Yee-hah!" The G squeals with glee, "Just check out the queens of the wild frontier. Woo-hooh wild boys! Spikey, it's the Wild West. Midnight cowboy country. Head 'em up, move 'em out... Rawhide geht alawng! I got no rim on my brown-eye, but I'm still mincing along. Wooh, dig those leather queens. Don't think much of yours Spike!"

"Oh, I don't know; cute butt."

I'm picking up G's infectious high spirit. G's cooking, and I'm getting hungry. This is how I like it to be. The Big City Beats. Tonight we're the mad, bad wordsmiths of E1. London legends, in search of... Who knows? Who cares? Tonight poetry is a wild beast, a hard bitch, a dominatrix, a strict mistress, clad in leather... Whip it on me Jim - just like Sister Ray said; just like the G tells it, and I want to believe him. Tonight I want to totally serve under the Muse's heel. I want to sacrifice myself before her altar. Tonight I'm a true believer, and I want to believe.

The truth is poetry isn't so much a wild beast as a queer fish. Truth is there ain't no fame, sex, or money in this scene. So why do we do it? It's a good question. Does it soothe the soul or calm the stresses of modern-day life? The emotional pains of mechanistic, masochistic, materialistic madness on 20th Century Street? Does it fuck. Perhaps we're men born out of time. Lily-livered fops who have no place in the big, bad city, or futurist warriors who will endeavour to survive the ultimate big bang, who's true mission is to have sufficient vision to make the new world a place fit for poets to live. Who knows? Why are we poets? Cos between us, me and G, we wanna believe we can say something. We have to believe we can say something. We have to believe that what we're doing is important. Maybe it is, maybe it isn't. I know in totalitarian regimes they imprison their poets. We aren't in a totalitarian regime, but we like to believe we're doing something dangerous. Me and the G, we make each other believe. Believe something is true, and it is true. Belief is a powerful thing; it's probably all that keeps a poet going when he's in prison - it's all that keeps a poet going when he's out of prison. I guess we also do it, believing one day we'll be famous and have plenty money... Who knows why we do it? Who gives a fuck?

Gene screams, "*I don't care too much for money// Money can't buy me love.* Oh I know I should have worn those leathers with the lace-up fly and detachable bum flap. Spike, whatever happened to those strides?"

The last time I'd seen those trousers was Gene walking away down Denmark Street shouting, "The White Brothers are over. We'll never make it as a rap band!"

Gene pulls up to the kerb, just outside the Colehurne, the renowned gay pub, with its profusion of pristine, gleaming Harleys and moustachioed leather queens. Heads turn as Gene shouts, "Let's rip it up baby, let's scream and shout!"

Hungry, sad, lecherous eyes pass over us, beckoning for us to stop a while, but we ain't here to flirt; we're here for our careers. In this city of spondulics where currency is king, and everyone knows you gotta pay to play, The Big City Beats, the commissars of the quatrain, are giving it away.

Two

We find the venue, The Troubadour, a little bistro full of badly dressed would-be bohos. We pass on, through the cappuccino-sipping pseudo intellectual clientele, and descend through a back entrance into a dank and decidedly dingy cellar. What are we doing here? No time for such dumb questions. Gene is deadly serious as he slowly surveys the denizens of this dimly-lit dungeon; a raggedly pack of chancers and no-hopers; the usual suspects we had come to expect: young and old hippies, care in the community exiles, pale students looking shy and withdrawn, every now and then scribbling into their notebooks. As I remember, they were thinly but evenly spread about, as if afraid to catch something - like a conversation with a stranger.

We stood at the back and watched for a while. The master of ceremonies was a misnomer, a bad case of someone performing as if they'd drawn the short straw and did not want to be next in front of the firing squad; as ever, only MCing at all, cos they'd organised the evening. Bad MCs were a perennial problem in this area of live entertainment; either they were motor mouth city, or just (like tonight's) plain bad. We watched. Actually, as I remember, a couple of the acts weren't half bad, but as ever they certainly weren't all good.

Poetry, such a strange phenomenon. Poetry, who needs it? It can be invigorating, it can be incredibly moving, but more often it can be as flaccid as a eunuch's dick, as dull as dishwater. Why was this? Many reasons: no focus, no hocus pocus, no wild youth, sex, fame or rock'n'roll.

Still, no time for analysis or therapy. Poetry in 80's Britain basically sucked; it was not vital. It was time for change. It was time for The Big City Beats. We were here, we were ready. We'd reconnoitred the opposition, we'd observed the situation, and realised the stark fact that the old jalopy poetry needed an overhaul, a new engine, some nuclear-injected fuel. We were suped-up, streamlined, and polished. We were what it needed, it didn't want us, there was no logic, but it needed a kick up the arse. Our boots had steel toe caps, and we were ready to do some serious stomping.

G had informed the compere of our intent, and told me we were going on after the act that was presently trying its best to capture the public imagination; a sad squeaky Melanie sound-a-like, who had already done too many tunes too many, and had lost what sympathy she'd begun with.

G turns to me and with a slow, steely rasp, says, "Well Spike, let's go to work."

There is a half-hearted ripple of applause as the cheese-clothed mousey blond folkster falters to the edge of the audience. The response is certainly not enough to warrant an encore, but she's vacillating; she will probably not have an opportunity to perform before a crowd for a long time and she's trying desperately to hang on to her brief entrance into the portals of the public domain.

G seizes his opportunity. He walks straight past her, takes the microphone off its stand, and declares, "One more round of applause please for our accomplished chanteuse".

They clap; slightly louder than they did before.

"My name's Gene Campbell, and I would like to introduce you to my partner of the spoken word, Spike Williams; and together we are **The Big City Beats!**"

Suddenly I feel the rush. The crystal clear flow as adrenaline flushes through my system. Panic! Can I remember the lines? The set? The body postures? Does this mean anything? Will people

To be read at 'The Special' gig 25.05.00

like us?

Gene is stood relaxed, serious. His hand outstretched, like some brave and gentle lifeguard, like the hand of God being offered to Adam on the roof of the Sistine Chapel. I know I will not drown. I know I am nothing, and yet I am incredibly important. Gene is relying on me. I will not let him down. It's time. Time to move from critique to action. Time not to wiggle a toe in the water, but to stretch out gloriously and swallow-dive into the maelstrom. No safety net, no parachute; caution was an encumbrance that we had long since flung over the side; excess baggage that we had voluntarily jettisoned way back at the beginning of our journey. It was time. We had paid our fare and the roller-coaster ride had already begun. No turning back. Feel the fear - feel the rush. First gig time. Like first sex. Love it or hate it, it only happens once. Our pants were down, our dicks erect. Virgin poets, ready for deflowering. Be gentle. Hell, be brutal, don't hold back, make us sore, lick every orifice and come over our faces. We are not victims. Sure we're scared but the smell in the air is not fear, it is the smell of desire. We wanna satisfy, we wanna see the audience orgasm. We believe we have the staying power, *we will make them come!*

I climb aboard the stage. Reality sandwich. Looking down, I gaze not upon hardcore lust. This audience looks like it's never had a hard-on - they look slack, limp - their only desire seems to be for their next cup of cocoa. But I'm here; **we're here!** And we mean business! Black suits, black turtlenecks, black shoes; a cross between sombre businessmen and Baader Meinhof. Word terrorists on a mission. The mission had begun. We operate as one; not slick, not machine-like, but each fully functioning as a complementary catalyst for the

It begins

other.

It all happened so fast. We paced the stage, like caged tigers, dangerous prisoners. Words strafed the night. Gesticulating hands, gyrating bodies, heads bobbing, eyes darting. No awkward silences or uncomfortable fidgets. Professionalism oozed from every pore. Metaphorically the warm blood and salty sweat dripped onto the boards. Our souls overspilled with emotion. Our poems breathed life into the room. Words ricocheted around the walls. Titles? "War of the Words", "Are You Tough Enough", "Sex", "Violence", "Mortality" all spring to mind. Our only props being our very existence and each other, oh yes, and a gun, which I had strapped in a shoulder holster under my jacket, which at a given moment I pulled out and pointed at the audience, who, hereto entranced, were transfixed in my sights, blank horror on their faces, as the shock and ultimate realisation of staring their executioners face-on. I knew it was fake (the gun that is), but the audience, who we had already stunned were mesmerised and entangled in the frenzied moment - they were willing victims; ready to believe; ready (if necessary) to die.

Like some psychopath about to flip into the ultimate blood bath, I moved to the front of the stage. I assumed the stance; a slight squat, legs akimbo, gun-hand clamped firmly in the other. Gene screamed my name. I shook my head slightly, as if to make the voices go away. Then I straightened up, and calmly turned the muzzle round, and placed the barrel in my mouth. The G rushed over and grabbed the revolver, pushed me to one side, and began a poem about going mental in the city called "Is it Me?" We didn't let up; not for an instant. We were watching awed amazement in the faces of our audience. Their quizzical expressions begged the questions: What is this? Who are these guys? Is the gun loaded? Are they loaded? Where do they come from? What are they on?

Nothing like us had ever happened to this place for years. Looks of puzzlement, anguish, anxiety, then... smiles. Like a release of pent-up emotion. Catharsis. A realisation that this was special, a happening in their neighbourhood. What they didn't know was that we'd rehearsed like a military platoon, we were battle hardened, no stage fright, we were ready. It was a pushover, a collision, but definitely no accident.

Once in an extraordinary while, you are a witness to something amazing happening in history, right before your eyes. All you can do is watch, and maybe in the future declare, "Yes, I was there!" but it's like some secret pact, or belonging to a clandestine order, only others who were witnesses themselves can really empathise. It's something you hold in your heart. Gene and I shared many such moments. We first crossed paths as two young punks in a Sex Pistols gig in Caerphilly 1976. There were more people outside protesting, than there were audience. It was frightening, it was thrilling, it was history in the making... **We were there.** I hope The Troubadour's audience felt like me and G did on that cold and hostile night in hicksville South Wales. I hope sometime in the future they'll meet someone else who mentions the Troubadour gig, and they can feel that warm glow as they say, "Yes, I was there."

It's true, you can't tell anyone anything they don't want to hear. I'm sure the poetry fraternity had had endless debates as their cappuccinos turned cold, reiterating the same old arguments as to why the scene was stale, stagnant. They knew it was an atrophied corpse. The undertaker had already embalmed the body and measured-up for a coffin. Then BANG! We arrived, out of nowhere, the emergency rescue. Scalpel, forceps, morphine. Masks at the ready. More oxygen, more oxygen. Pump it, pump it! Give this stiff a shot of adrenaline. WHAM! Slapping the pallid cheek, giving it the kiss of life, tongues down its throat, fingers down its pants, to feel the first twitch of the rising hard-on. For one night at least, the dead rose, jumped and jived. Like zombies in Michael Jackson's "Thriller", the cancerous cadaver was doing the Moonwalk, the terminally ill patient of poetry had not only picked up its blanket to walk, it was fucking break-dancing; spinning on its head. Just for once the hanged-man ate a hearty breakfast, dangled at the end of death, experiencing the most amazing ejaculation, and lived to tell the tale. The condemned convict happily left the cell on death row, to settle into the hot seat, and smiled while 12,000 volts coursed through every nerve end. Just for tonight poetry was fantastically, electrically alive.

End of set.

G is stood at my side. I feel great. I'm satisfied. Full of the knowledge that we came and conquered. A feeling that we were good, very good, hot to trot, the business. It's not often you get that feeling, when you do something and you don't have to ask, or seek a reaction, because you know deep down, **Damn I'm good.** Maybe that's all there is. We struggle and strive for that moment to say ***Damn I'm good!*** Is it the meaning of life? Hell, what do I know? But it's a start, something to hold on to, to grasp; and when it's gone, you recollect your thoughts, pick yourself up, dust yourself off, and get ready for the next assault in the battle called life. Maybe, for people like me and the G, life could only be lived knowing there was a reason - and the reason was, to reach that point of doing and saying, and more importantly *knowing* ... **DAMN I'M GOOD**. I had many of those moments with Gene; that's why I'm still looking, needing more. As the song goes, *Catch a falling star and put it in your pocket// Never let it fade away*. That first gig, we cut our hands catching that star. We were bloodied, smiling, pockets bulging, determined to move on, but we had grasped the impossible - we had experienced the heavenly light.

I'm stood next to G, just bathing in the glory of it all. They are applauding loudly. Then suddenly Gene shouts, "Your best is not enough!"

He stands on an empty chair in the front row. "Your best will never be good enough!"

He steps over row after row. People are scrabbling to avoid his mad onslaught. He barrages his way to the back, then he's storming up the stairs. Heads are turned; mouths agog.

I'm stood there, hands in the air. I'm angry. I'm embarrassed. I'm stood here. Gene's gone. The seconds slowly tick in silence. Gene has gone. I don't know what to do. Then somebody claps. Then another, and another. The applause mounts. Heads are turning towards me, then back to the exit. Maybe they think if they clap loud enough the G will return, and they will have some grand finale. Gene has definitely disappeared. The applause continues to rise. This is insane - this is magnificent. I raise a fist, and as the clapping subsides, I shout, "You have just witnessed The Big City Beats. Ladies and gentlemen - goodnight!"

Three

Our first gig as the Big City Beats. I caught a tube as far as Tower Hill - it was the last tube - I wanted to go to Bow - I walked home. It started raining. I walked along the Whitechapel Strip. I thought of Travis in "Taxi Driver" hoping one day the rain would come and wash the scum off the streets. Whitechapel High Street had seen many a heavier downpour than the one I was experiencing that night. Whitechapel High Street would experience many more downpours. Whitechapel High Street would still be there long after I'd been washed down the drain. Our first gig over, and that was that. A walk home down the Mile End Road, alone, in the rain. Gene wasn't with me to tell me it all made sense. Gene had his own disappointments to deal with, his own dreams that turned to nightmares. I want to thank Gene for showing me some of his dreams..... but that night I wanted to punch his head in - the inconsiderate bastard - walking away and leaving me.... **How dare he!**

I was tamping. I got home soaked through, with sore feet. I rang Gene straight away. The answer machine droned that nobody was available. The next day, I rang four times - the same message - I raged to the machine. The days went by - I rang less often - my rage subsided to anger - then on the third day of pathetic angry messages, I pleaded to his machine that I was really worried, and could he just ring to say he's OK? - He didn't!

Four

See a light, a neon light, crease your eyes like a Chinese, watch the sodium light rays sever, laser sharp into the dark oblivion. Keep with it, fix on it, move with it, be it, see the lines merge with other strips of yellow and white. Neon light bondage wrapping its tentacles, shooting its way through the deep blackness to the even deeper blackness within, a darkness that hides the other side, the horror, the strange, the bizarre and hideous, the dark, dark side of ourselves that needs to be hid.

What does happen in those disgusting dark alleyways, in the labyrinthine lanes of sordid love and late night lust of back against the wall brainfucks? You *say* you don't really want to know, but you *think* you may really like to take a peek. I'm a voyeur myself, I guess; I suppose it goes with the territory of late night TV consumption, where we all become voyeurs, critics, and opinionated observers. Me? I'm a sight for sore eyes. Be careful, be gentle with me - ooh baby don't, pull it out, don't come, don't come... no, no, no! Yes! Tears mingle with sweat; what you didn't want you wanted most, and that's what you got - and now it's over. Hopes are dashed on the rocks. The cobbled streets of E1, full of trash, broken glass... SNAP, CRACK! *Get the fuck together Spike. What are you doing here?*

"Dreamer, dreamer, queen screamer, rim and reamer," squeals Rhys; the blond, pale shitbag, a neurosis and crisis-ridden scumbag. The Aryan super-model schizo with absolutely no common sense and no terms of reference. He really was the dead weight jetsam that somehow kept bobbing among the flotsam of life. Rhys was supposed to be enrolled on some sort of fashion design course, but was definitely not designing anything. Sure he had a great selection of suits, but he had a threadbare mind and lots of frayed ends. The most you could admire was that miraculously he was still hacking it, faking it. I could say he was a real ducker and diver but that would imply he had the intelligence to fashion some kind of game plan; if he had it was some distressed and twisted fabric, some tattered tactic that could spin more sub-plots and weave more elaborate webs than a Hitchcock movie.

What can I say about Rhys? He was the carrion of humankind; a vulture waiting for a free lunch, waiting for the next relative to die and leave him some money. So far he'd succeeded - he'd received two lots of cash from his dearly departed, and he was waiting for more. Not that he had a massive amount of relatives, and none of the remaining looked particularly unwell.

Rhys - What a state! - yearning for real estate - someone - anyone, who could leave him anything - a little something to help him get by. It doesn't work; Rhys blows whatever he gets within a few months, on hookers and alcohol. Lord, he'd blow me, if I could give him some money. Rhys only moves for moolah, otherwise he don't twitch a muscle - he goes through life imitating a lazy salamander. He even keeps small lizards in a glass cage in his barren flat; they're perfect pets for the Rhys, no fuss, and they're not exactly going to break your neck with their agile acrobatics. I've sat and looked at those lizards, just static, except for the slow moving tongue, and tried to conceive of what might go on inside their reptilian brains: not much, not much as far as I could see, they just give me the creeps with their complete inactivity, until they want to eat, then *BLAM!* they catch a cricket in the blink of an eye.

What goes on inside Rhys' head? Maybe the lizards know. It's probably as empty as his flat - no clutter or lived-in look - austere, tidy, everything precise and precious in its place - but not clean; a veneer of dust, a smear of grime. Someone like Rhys should be a psychiatrist's dream, such a patient would seem like a goldmine, to a caring psychiatric community - only in E1, there are so many Rhys-type people, nobody cares. What can Community Care do, when the community is as fucked-up as the patient?

I don't really want to delve too deep into the mental miasma of Rhys. Hell we all have our problems, he just has more than most. Rhys was strictly a junk-free person, if you discounted hash (and it seemed everyone was toking spliff in those days), so he wasn't an addict, not until the NHS psychiatric system got hold of him. He liked to think he was a serious drinker - he carried his dad's old pewter hip flask in his back pocket - but it was all a facade; like everything about Rhys, the outside was passable if all you were doing was having a quick peek as you passed by - but what went on inside his head?...

"Light a beacon with a Puerto Rican," Rhys cackles.

"What the fuck you talking about, you scumbag, you don't know any Puerto Ricans," I shout.

"I want to be in America, everything's free in America," Rhys squeals and does a little jig, stamping his feet as if he's wearing cha-cha heels. He does a mock pirouette, unzips his fly and takes out his cock. "Hee, hee, hee - suck it and see."

"Jesus Rhys! Put it away, you fuckhead schizo - just tell me, where is G?"

"Are you talking to me?" says Rhys looking down at his cock in his full length mirror. "Cos I ain't no schizo. Maybe he is, or they are," he says pointing around at no-one in particular. He's wiggling his dick around. "Ooh, so charming, prince charming, so... what?"

I stand up, make a fist, and bring it close to Rhys' face. "Rhys stop fucking with me. Where's G?"

"Ooh really!" He shrieks and runs off into his bedroom.

"Awh Rhys sorry, don't be..."

He appears out of the bedroom brandishing a Gurkha knife. He stops in front of me holding the knife in both hands, the point touching my fly. I am frightened.

"Ooh eeh - such a fucking tuffy."

This guy is deranged and potentially dangerous. What have I done? What am I going to do? I hate myself. I hate violence. I hate violence most cos I'm crap at it. Usually it ends up with me kissing boot leather, or nursing knuckle sandwich bruises. In my fantasies I'm Bruce Lee, I'm Judge Dredd... I'm don't fuck with me muthafucka. But, constantly, reality pushes in on me like some pissed off rhinoceros, like a drunken bouncer kicking several shades of shite out of an innocent punter...

Reality for me at this moment is a schizo psycho drama queen wielding a big fucking blade, pointed directly at my dick. I would love to take control with some fantastic Kung Fu high kick, and clout him real good; make him cry, make him beg on his knees for mercy. Instead I meekly say, "Please stop it Rhys, you shouldn't fool around."

Rhys laughs with glee, "Hee, hee, hee. You were really kacking it then, Mister Big Deal Macho. Wonder how you'd feel with eighteen inches of cold steel shoved up your shitter."

I laugh a nervous laugh. Rhys just puts the kukri down on the coffee table, picks up a cigarette, lights it and takes a big draw. I slump down onto the most uncomfortable aluminium chair. I figure it's some kind of deferential gesture to let Rhys know he's won.

Rhys is stood posing in the mirror taking big drags on his Benson, while posturing in profile.

Jeez, why do I constantly find myself in the presence of crazees? Do I enjoy being in fear of my life? In my fantasy I can take it - mortal combat - no holds barred - but reality?... I hate reality. I don't feel properly equipped to cope with the amount of hard work required, just to get by, just to survive. I certainly don't feel I've been given the right tools for the job. Sometimes I think I'm a man out of time. I mean I can't swim, ride a bike, drive a car, hold onto a girlfriend. The twentieth century is definitely not for me. This isn't self loathing, or self pity - or maybe it is - either way, in E1 it's no use looking for the sympathy vote.

Reality - why doesn't it go away, or freeze

frame for a moment, a good moment. There's real time and reel time; everyone wants to be a star and be in the movies, but the reality of my life is a movie nobody would want to see; the script is crap, the acting abominable, the set is being dismantled before my eyes, and if there is a plot, then I can't follow it.

Dodgy, I feel dodgy. I feel I've been dealt a hand of dodgy cards, and the rule (if there is any) is you've got to play with what you got. I'm fucked, but hell I'm sure Rhys is getting more fucked; I think his set is either missing a few cards, or is full of jokers. God, I shouldn't criticise - I know he's had a rough deal. I'll tell you about it sometime. Fuck, who am I? Mr. Mother Theresa? We've all had bum deals - we've all had hard lives - I've just had to calm a mad psycho with a Gurkha knife! I long for an age when things were simpler, easier. *Man out of time get fucking real, most of your problems you brought about yourself* - I mean at least I wasn't forced up chimneys when I was a kid. Remember the good old days? Actually no, and I don't think they were that fucking good. Enjoy yourself when you're young - well I'm young now - I feel like a thousand years old.

Something's got to give, if you ask me. As you're not, I'm gonna say my piece anyways - no one listens, but you've got to shout, or say something so startlingly frank, honest and brilliant, that it's dazzling - where everyone stops and says in unison, "Why didn't we think of that?" As the startlingly frank moments are as rare to me as the chance of catching two dodos fucking on prime time TV, I guess I'll just keep shouting until I'm hoarse.

Oh God, what's the reasoning you're using here Spike? No-one gives a fuck, if I'm screaming my views from the roof tops.

Everyone is pursuing their own course, everyone has their own way of seeing and doing. Horses for courses. Some people are jockeying in the fast track. Me? I'm stuck here in E1, a one horse town, headed straight for the knacker's yard. All living careers toward death; the final finishing post. Life's a bitch and then you die, Gene always says. Where the fuck is G?

"Rhys where's Gene?" I implore. I fix him with the most penetrating stare I can muster - compelling him to give me an answer.

"Shan't, can't, won't," says Rhys, in the most queenie voice it disgusts.

"Look Rhys, don't be unkind. It's not Mastermind. Where is he?"

"Oh, around. A round peg in a square hole. You know G, he can't quite fit in anywhere."

"You mean a square... oh forget it. Look, just tell me when you last saw him!" I plead.

"You really want to know? You really want the truth - the whole truth - so help me God?" Rhys crosses his heart (if he's got one), and places his hands in mock prayer.

"Yes, yes, yes, anything," I gasp.

"Well, let me see... when was it...? Oh yes, last Friday, out in the courtyard, giving some sweets to kids... Some very nasty sweets... Some kids who should have been old enough to know better. Ooh eeh, it was trick or treat - you know - the treats with a trick that make you sick, leave you wanting for more." Rhys talks in his monotone staccato style.

Sometimes I think Rhys is a robot; a screwed-up, malfunctioned machine, that somehow escaped from the assembly line, before the finer adjustments were finally made. Was he brought up, moulded, or mashed into existence? Whatever the truth, the traces are concealed within the labyrinthine corridors called his mind. Ask a straight question, and what do you get? Convoluted and obscure gibberish! Why do I bother? What am I even here for? I'm here to see if Rhys can help me with the whereabouts of G.

Gene used to live here in the Grove, where the Rhys now resides. He left a couple of years ago, after he'd been busted twice in close succession. The last time, he had his door kicked down by seven burly DS from Scotland Yard. He went to court, but was never convicted of anything. I never found out the full story. He moved out shortly after, into a tower block in Stepney. Access was harder on the thirteenth floor, with intercoms and security cameras on the main doors. I'd called round there several times on my way home from work. I'd buzzed long and hard... No reply. I could see the lights were on, it really didn't mean much, Gene always left the lights on. I suspected he was home. I'm here cos I'm a desperate poetry junky; one half of the Big City Beats. I can't do anything without G. Where is he?

"Hey, have I shown you these beautiful pictures of these Thai babes I got from an agency?" Rhys side-tracks. He's holding a bunch of colour photographs.

Rhys who has never had much luck with women had a scam of bringing over Thai girls, and either marrying them, or getting them into his own porn movies. Of course this was all in his fucked-up head, but he had the pictures. You act, and there are consequences. Rhys had acted. I just hoped to God the photos remained fodder for his meat beating fantasies, and no poor Thai woman would end up with this demented specimen.

"What do you mean 'treats'?..." Rhys wasn't going to tell me anything real. "Oh just forget it!" I snap.

I was getting up to go, when Rhys spoke in a low, steady tone.

"You know the trouble with you Spike?" he purred. This was déjà vu. I expected the same old sadistic wit, after being told what a sad git I was, and it all ending with some high pitched cackle, as Rhys giggled at his own sarcastic snipes.

"You know the trouble with you Spike?"

I waited impatiently, for the usual intolerant doggerel - the gospel according to el supremo sad fuck. He seemed unbelievably calm, but the blade was still in front of him, so I figured it was best to placate him and wait for the unsound logic of the lunatic to spout forth.

"You know the trouble with you Spike, is you're always looking for a silver lining. You're blinded by the shiny glare, but you should have realised by now, there's nothing there. There is no silver lining, no exit light at the end of the long corridor. Life is one big fucked-up mess. It's darkness.

It's horror. It's a long line of all those strangers your parents told you not to talk to. They'll fuck you up - fuck you over - abuse you and pass you down the line. Life is buggered and bleeding in a child care centre, with some social worker wiping the spunk and blood off the sheets to try and hide the dirty deed. Spike, the trouble with you is you're a dreamer. You're looking for the treasure at the end of the rainbow, and in the end... it turns out to be a crock of shit. Visions are for visionaries. Spike, you ain't no visionary - you're just a sad idealist. Get real Spike. You're a civil servant with a silly socialist viewpoint. Dreams are for dreamers. Wake up Spike, and welcome to the nightmare. Wise up guy, cos it's all there is; this is it Spike baby, it ain't going to get any better - in fact its going to get a lot worse. And you know..." Rhys pouted.

"Wha?" I stupidly ask, completely taken aback that Rhys can string together more than one sentence.

"And you know... no-one gives a fuck whether you live or die - not really. As old Zen Buddha would say, you are a mere speck, bobbing on the surface of the cosmic sea, and the shit-filled tidal wave is barrelling out of the sewer, coming along to crush the life out of you, and drag you under. So get on that surfboard and surf baby, surf." Rhys ended, taking a swig from his hip flask, as he drunkedly kissed his photographs of Thai women.

What is it about mad people? There's all those crazy connections inside their heads that almost convince you they are touched by some rare insights beyond the veil of reality. *What the fuck am*

I thinking? Mad people are mad. Rhys spent 18 months in St.Clements, the local loony bin. They sectioned him, cos he was hearing voices which told him to kill children - he thought he had killed children. Why throughout my life do I find myself involved with mad people? Where's G?
"Bang kok," says Rhys. "Bang, bang - Cocky, cocky."

Five

Six days later I came home from work - Gene had rung that afternoon and left a message saying we should get together to rehearse; we had a gig at the Chelsea Arts & Crafts Fair at the Old Town Hall, Kings Road, in three days time. No apologies. No explanations. Nothing! I felt so relieved - then I felt angry. I wanted to punish him; give him a dose of his own medicine. It went through my head that I wouldn't ring him back immediately - I rang him 3 minutes later.

Six

"Why should we walk when we can fly?//Onwards, upwards, towards tomorrow, towards the sky!" we shouted at our own reflections.

We were in G's living room on the 13th floor of Bradmore House, an asbestos sixties high-rise, staring intently into the full-length that covered a whole wall, gesticulating wildly, pointing towards the ceiling; slightly cracked and white, like the local residents I thought. Yes, why should we walk? We had a dream, a vision, that gave us wings. I looked hard at the mirror. Have you ever looked.... I mean a long, hard, intense look, into the mirror? Looking as if trying to reach beyond the mere reflection?

My grandmother said to me when I was little, "If you look too long into the mirror, you'll see the devil."

Once when I was eight I did it, and I really did - I'm positive - I saw the devil. He had a pointy chin, hair, and he was red, but even then I thought it was just my imagination - a vision.

Now I'm older, and what do I see? Two grown-up men in their late twenties, posing, preening, jumping and shouting. Two obsessed madmen. Two devils in a hell called Stepney. Two prophets in an urban hell hole dreaming dreams of Gods.

This was no RADA school for would-be thespians; maybe the theatre of hard knocks, down some dark and dangerous alley, at the end of Lonely Street. Bradmore House was no ivory tower for emaciated dreamers - it was a hardcore concrete and asbestos high-rise built on 60's high hopes and ideals in London's East End. The area had a rich history (of poverty) from Jack The Ripper to the Krays - and in-between bombed to oblivion in World War II - at least then the Blitz destroyed the slums; and in their place? Buildings sprouting upward; moderne and climbing to the sky - a Bauhaus model of utility and function for the working masses. From back-to-backs to watch your back - don't open the door to strangers. Broken housing schemes, broken dreams, busted ideals. Community spirit is a hard drink at the local. Piss in the lifts and swastikas on the walls. 1940's to 1980's - the dream of a land fit for heroes fades, but we have a dream - we're The Big City Beats, we dream cos dreaming is free.

Thirteen floors up in Bradmore and I can see Canary Wharf; that monument to Manhattan architecture. Rising up out of the waterfront wasteland of the Isle of Dogs. Some hate it. Is it a grand folly, to remind us of Thatcherite madness, or is it a cruel joke, in which the financiers will have the last laugh? I love it - it shines high on my East End horizon, its clean and clear design is such a distinct difference from my E1 metropolis. Who cares what it means; how much it cost? It's a brave statement in a world full of veiled half truths and insidious lies, its very existence declares its intent. It says, "Look I am here - look at me."

Meanwhile back in the mirror, what do I see? Two men rehearsing their dream, their statement, their art. Two soldiers drilling for a war that has not yet been declared. Two strangers in a strange land. Two outsiders, born out of time, on the wrong planet. It's choreographed, but it's not dance, unless we're doing the E1 front-line two step. It's art, but we have no pallet of colours or blocks of stone to fashion our statement of immortality, and no museums to purchase us for posterity. It's The Big City Beats; two desperate, wannabe poets, looking into the mirror, rehearsing their passing reflections on life, strife and the obscene that is our adopted home; the Big Smoke. London, so bad they named it once. Hell, it's where we live, it's home, it's where the heart and the hurt meet. Stepney, where pearly kings and queens swagger in mock majesty, down streets paved with fool's gold. Where pure bred cockney Staffs and Rottweilers would love a chance to eat imposters like us, up for breakfast. This urban paranoia is part of the high octane fuel that keeps our engines turning - nerves shot, hopes higher than Tim Leary on LSD. Burroughs' bike boys don't hang out too long in Stepney. There's only one Queen and they all wave their Union Jack on her birthday, God save her. Still looking in the mirror at a transient reflection, still searching for The Big City Beats.

On the left is me. Hi, I'm Keith, or Spike as people often call me. It's a nickname that's stuck since I was fourteen in Pontypridd Boys' Grammar School. It's funny how you accept a situation almost without thinking. I never wondered how I managed to get into school, I certainly didn't think I was anything special, or different. Most of my mates went to secondary school, and I knew they were being lined-up for the factory gates. The best grammar offered was grooming for the supervisor's role at the same factory. Fuck that; as options, as aspirations, both stank.

"Schooldays; the best days of your life," my Dad used to say. Maybe. Maybe for him, but I'm sure you don't look at it that way if your head's pushed down the toilet and you're constantly being bullied. Don't get me wrong, I wasn't a particular victim or scapegoat, or bully for that matter; I was just part of that vast middle morass of boys learning to be boys, learning how to survive, learning how to clout - test their strength - putting it about. I just got through the situation I found myself in, same as everyone else. The big bad world didn't beckon us; in truth it was mainly ignored. Fuck knows where or when I began to understand that the pen is mightier than the sword. I'm not sure (even now) if I believe it is.

"What do you want to be when you grow up?" asked the careers teacher. We called him Jiminy Cricket, because he looked remarkably like the cartoon character. But a physical likeness was where the resemblance ended. Truth is he didn't possess an ounce of the sense that cartoon Jiminy displayed. He emitted a feeling of despair and failure in his class that seemed to entrap us like insidious fog. We could see that he had drawn the short straw in being the careers teacher, and like us, he didn't want to be there.

I remember, in the last year, when we were in transition to become a comprehensive, and we had girls in school; one of them, in Jiminy's class, stood up proudly and said, "I want to be an actress". Silence. Then from Jiminy there followed a long catalogue of barriers and obstructions as to why this was not a serious option for a young girl. You name it, he said it; rattling off a list that included, unemployment, lack of security, small parts for women, his objections went on and on, with an overwhelming implication that there was something seedy and very unladylike about such a profession. By the end, the girl had slumped back down in her chair, and like the rest of us, felt dejected and rejected. For Jiminy, his rule of thumb was, why sow seeds of encouragement when you can sow seeds of doubt.

One boy yelled he wanted to be an astronaut. Jiminy dismissed this without a comment. I said "careers teacher." It sparked a small laugh in class and got me detention. The starting blocks of my brilliant career were super-glued, a poet was nowhere in my scheme of things. I didn't know what I wanted to be. Life was one big road, with a hell of a gradient, going upwards to God knows where. I just knew I had to get on the bus and take my chances on the tarmac. The only good thing about growing up in a small town is it's easier to find a bigger one to go to. I got on the bus.

The nickname? Oh, that was nothing special, wild, or romantic. Many times I had tried to dress it up, like I had come from a long line of assassins - but I always ended up telling the boring truth. Some fat kid at school laughed at my Aladdin Sane hairstyle and said, "You look like a porcupine. I'm going to call you Spike." I thought nothing of this remark, but news travelled fast, and the name stuck. I wasn't bothered, he could have called me "Shitface."

Spike Williams. When Gene met me I was

Spike, and that's what he always called me.

Let's not talk about me. This isn't really my story. I was there. I was a witness. I'm trying to understand what happened. I'm trying to piece together what happened to Gene; my compadre, mon amis. Morecambe had his Wise, Ronnie his Reggie. Me? I got Gene - or he got me. Was there a choice? "Life," as Bogey said, "don't amount to a hill of beans, in this crazy world." Hey, but it's all we got. I got you babe - you - Gene Campbell, one half of the Big City Beats; the would-be duo taking on the world's mysteries and looking for...? ...some kicks and meaning?

Some people you bump into, some just string along, some become like Siamese twins - not physically, but spiritually. Look I'm not going to get all metaphysical or religious. Here I am again, looking in the mirror, rehearsing for the next show, and maybe it's time I stared a little bit harder, a little bit deeper; penetrate that image that reflects from the surface, and look further; into our inner beings, our lives. We only get one shot - it's not a rehearsal - what do I see?

Gene - I'd known him on and off, for ten years. I had a picture, but there were still gaps. I'd known him, but still I couldn't say I'd covered all the angles, all the points. He was like an electric eel; slippery and shocking. I have never cared to be judgmental, life's too short, too hypocritical. I was never sure how firm my own ground was, to be shooting holes in others' lifestyles. Life was too complicated to choose blinkered tunnel vision. When I met G, it suited me fine, all I had to do was hold on tight, and climb aboard for the ride. It was a dodgy vehicle, the journey was sometimes scary and bumpy, but it was MOVING, LIVING. "Strap yourself in, hang on to your hats. Here we go!" ....**WHOOSH!!** Wow, that was close!

Gene - some said he was a drug dealer, operating in a shadowy world on the dark edge of town. Born in Patagonia, learnt art from Warhol, prose from Kerouac, poetry from Ginsberg. He was gay, bisexual, a hot hetro in the sheets. Some say he was a monk, Buddhist, celibate, wise and deeply spiritual. Others thought him a fraud, a shaman, conman, a shyster, a grifter; a fixer who could get anything done, for you, or to you, a trickster who looked after number one. They said there was nothing he wouldn't do to get what he wanted, that he had no morals or scruples. They warned me he was a real bad ass, and I'd best keep well away. It was rumoured that he was the kid who left a Northern town at fifteen to become a rent boy, touting for business in the amusement arcades off the Dilly. Others, that he'd hung out in New York leather bars, being buggered and abused, giving head to anyone and everyone. Or there was the story, that he'd been picked up by some lonely middle-aged, rich, New York widow, who'd taken him in Pygmalion stylee, and preened and primed him into the confident Paul Newman character he is today. They say he still sees her and screws her occasionally, and that's where he gets his cash. And one malicious gossip, that proclaimed he had proof, insisted that sometimes G had her and her daughter together, in the same bed. He's driven a Cadillac on Sunset

Boulevard, and hitched from East to West coast on every continent. Some say he's a schizo/psycho, a Don Juan with a string of lovers around the globe, a girl and guy in every port. To others he's full of bullshit; a low-life fag gigolo who'd sell his ass for a dime. Opinions, opinions.......

.... I was on the Mile End Road. I was having a curry in the Passage To India with an old friend from Wales, Gareth Jones. Gareth had known Gene from the past; way before I knew him. I was talking about Gene and the conflicting accounts around his history. I couldn't believe what happened next. The atmosphere suddenly changed. I raised my head - shocked. I looked Gareth in the eyes, he was shaking with rage,

"Well if you want to know the truth," he blurted, "his dad was a bus conductor. He went to secondary school in Whitby or Whitley Bay, or some such shite Northern town. He studied architecture at Leeds Poly but never made a degree. The only time he's been out of the country was on a package tour."

I was reeling.

I got to my feet. "I have to go now."

I put £10 on the table and walked towards the door; my head was spinning. It wasn't from his bitter little version of the truth, but his gratingly pathetic, venomous whine, his uncontrolled outburst of envy. His jealous lack of respect. His story - his personal version of the G's history didn't mean anything to me - I'd heard so many versions before - none of them <u>really</u> tallying - none of them convincing. I'd heard some shocking, and plenty, like his, ridiculously mundane. Somehow, everyone's opinion (and it seemed everyone had an opinion), only added to the myth; only raised G's status. Gareth would like to believe that Gene never accomplished anything, but deep down he was ridiculously envious.

I didn't know who to believe. To me Gene *was* a star - yes a shooting star - destined to burn up - leaving no real impact or trace. Gene was a hero, at a time in history when the only heroes were in movies. Gene was a hero in an age when fashion had no real time for heroes. Gene couldn't stand to be alone - always the lone hero. The world could not give him what he needed - the world was not capable of such support. I couldn't give him what he needed - he needed people with bigger dreams than me. I bathed in the glow, help stoke the inferno, but ultimately all I could really do was stand by and watch as dreams fired-up in heaven, fuelled by hell, burned out in limbo, leaving a pile of ash. I just couldn't see why people needed to piss on the embers.

I have my own recollection. Once at the beginning of our brief poetry career, before we'd begun writing or rehearsing, when me and the G were both drunk and stoned in a seedy gay bar in South Soho, Gene started raving about how famous we were going to become, he was going on about how we would make it to the very top by whatever means necessary.

I glibly asked Gene, "How low would you go?"

He replied, "Lower. Much much lower!"

I really don't think it had all that profound an effect on me at the time, through the chemically induced haze, but it's a memory that lingers; it's a recurring scenario now, in my dreams. It was the way G's face changed from devil-may-care, to absolute deadly serious. Yes, I do believe Gene had walked through the dark valley - he didn't make a big issue out of it - he didn't make any kind of an issue out of it at all - it was his face, his hand gestures, the aura he carried. Yes, I do believe he was a player in a dodgy game; an actor on this broadest of stages - it's just the role he'd been cast was a little more dramatic than most.

What's my line? Well maybe Gene was all, or none of the things people said. We've all got our histories. I don't criticise or rationalise; really I don't care. Gene was a man - my friend. All I know is our lives have crossed more times than cars on Spaghetti Junction. I don't really know if I believe in fate, but I think G and me were fated; we just kept on bumping into each other; drawn like moths to the same flame. God knows there have been times when I thought we'd never see each other again, but something always ensured we were bound together for at least some of this mad journey.

Life - funny how it moves and grooves.

Look, as I see it, his story is history; I can't change it, and what he's done, or where he's been is very important, but ultimately immaterial. All I know is that we've been through some scrapes; we'd made it to here, a living room in Stepney - looking in the mirror - and now I'm left; still searching for the Big City Beats.

I'm staring at G's reflection, and suddenly realise that Gene's looking at me. "Spike, as you've obviously decided to leave the rehearsal, I'd like to take the opportunity to tell you something very important that's happened to me... I've met somebody, her name's Maria..."

He told me he was happy for the first time in ages. He told me he was in love. Then suddenly the oddest expression drifted across his face. It's as if I wasn't there, as if he was alone, and he turned to the mirror, and in a strange, drawn-out moment of prophecy and intense sadness, he spoke out loud to his own reflection: "Poor Gene. Poor, poor Gene."

Then, before I could question, he snapped into a different mode. He saw something in that mirror. Maybe he saw some kind of devil, like I'd seen all those years ago. Whatever it was, he suddenly shook his head, he shuddered, then he altered his face, his expression, his posture, back to the G he wanted to see - back to the G he wanted me to see.

"Right Spike, and once more, from the top, *Sex, well slide some skin on me...!*"

Seven

I'm walking from Sloane Square tube. I remember when the Costello song "I Don't Want To Go To Chelsea" came out, and I knew exactly what it meant - I was young then, and thought I knew something - I was stupid - a stupid young punk with an adopted attitude. Me and my mate John Davies would travel all the way from Pontypridd just so we could see and be seen on the Kings Road on a Saturday. We'd walk up, then cross over the road and walk down, with what we presumed was a menacing swagger and a fuck off panache - God it was boring. Now, same as then (if only I was honest enough to have admitted it) part of me would love to stay here in Chelsea - belong here - strut up and down the Kings Road and admire and be admired by all the beautiful people. Now, as then, it certainly has its pull on me, like some powerful magnetic forcefield, and me the tiny metal filing, but the power is wealth; the magnetism of money, money I do not have. I could never really fit in, and even though I would like to pretend that maybe one day... But what's the point? If you know you don't fit in, there's really not much point in pretending. My working class socialist ancestry does not make me qualified to ever really belong - they could never really accept me. I cringe when I think of those Saturdays in the late 70's... No there's nothing worse than trying to fit in, and looking like a complete prat in the process. God, it's quite sad when one gets older and realises more just how the classes are divided in this country. I mean, even if I did make it and I hung out in all the right places declaring, "Hey, I've arrived!" the resounding retort would be, "But, dharling, we know where you've come from!" I guess I'm just a working class sheep shagger at heart.

Maybe my perception says a lot about me, but it seems on the Kings Road there's plenty mutton dressed as lamb, and I'm one of them. All this goes through my head as I walk towards the Old Town Hall. I'm dressed all in black and it's July. I feel hot and shoddy. My suit is a woollen dress suit from Oxfam - one of those with the satin trim down the pant seam. I don't know much about which designer labels I should be wearing, but Moss Bros. is definitely not one of them. I wish I was with Gene, I know he'd have something to say that would make this into some sort of logical sense, but Gene was going to meet me at the venue, he had business in West London.

As I approach the Old Town Hall I can see Gene, my stomach wells with a wonderful feeling of relief – it's all going to be alright. Gene doesn't see me, he's stood outside the gig with a beautiful woman at his side. He's wearing shades, so's she, they're smoking. Gene doesn't look ill at ease, or hot or bothered - he looks incredibly cool and confident - he looks like he belongs, they both do. He's wearing a black suit made of linen or something - he's slightly tanned - how does he manage that? Maria - cos obviously this must be his new found love - looks tanned, but she's Italian, she looks it; chic, expensive clothes, lots of gold, classy but not bawdy. Black hair in an immaculate bob, dark glasses, heavy red lipstick on full lips, she smokes her cigarette as if she's giving a blow job - she oozes sensuality - a look but don't touch - an interesting mix of virgin nun and hot sex tramp - I didn't understand what her attraction was for Gene, I could see what G's attraction was for her. She looked dangerous.

Gene turns and sees me approaching. "Hey

Spikey, good to see you guy - looking good, looking good. This is Maria, I told you about her."

So I'm right up against Maria, she extends her hand saying, "Ah, zo you must be zee Spike?" and giggles, a kind of deep throaty, voluptuous giggle. Her hand is held out towards me, but in such an indolent way, I wasn't sure whether she was intending I should shake it or kiss it, so I gripped it softly and raised it to my lips. She pulled her hand away and laughed, embarrassed. Gene made no comment. Maria looked disdainful, I felt stupid and nobody said anything to ease the situation. Then G threw his cigarette to the ground, squashed it under his sole, and said "Let's go reconnoitre."

Inside, the stalls looked over-dressed with exorbitant price tags, exactly like the punters - still the Fair was a place to be seen, a social barometer for the Chels set, everyone looked frightfully interested in the goods being sold, and the air was awash with money and light banter. Gene began laughing as our way was barred by an old couple with a pink poodle; he wore a pale blue safari suit and purple cravat, she a red feather boa and blond wig, they were haggling over the price of a cerise snake-skin Filo Fax. I got a distinct feeling that people felt they had to be seen buying something daring, something glitzy, trashy or boho, just so they could enter in to the brave world of luxury consumption for it's own sake - even if what they bought ended up in the charity shop next week.

Waste, the ultimate testament to true wealth. Not that I'm in any real position to be a knowledgeable critic. Gene used to say, "I've had money, and I've had none... Having it was definitely better." He's probably right. Maria looked completely at ease with it all - I bet she was here last year.

We found the stage, a raised rostrum in the middle of the stalls, about five feet high, so it was more or less visible from a good thirty feet away. At present there was some new age bollocks band; wind chimes, violins and some fat middle-aged frump in a orange muslin tent dress, grinning inanely and singing in Bulgarian, or some such esoteric Eastern European language. We stood right in front and watched a while. Gene, his arms folded across his chest, rocked on his heels and glowered, Maria did a beautiful job of looking incredibly bored, and I began feeling nervous. But I loved this pre-gig nerve-game time, when we psyched out the opposition, geeing ourselves up mentally into the gang mentality of The Big City Beats.

I asked Gene when we were on, only to be told there was no real schedule, we just had to take the stage, hit them hard and take no prisoners. This seemed to be getting the regular line with G, all combative verbals, as if we were the self-appointed SAS of the poetry corps. His battle plan for regaining lost terrain was some strategy, but ultimately required (like any warfare) a huge dollop of force.

As I'm writing this, I can see how ridiculous it all seems now, but I was a more-than-willing volunteer recruit, who thrilled to G's clarion call. Maybe it's got something to do with my lack of fisticuff skills - maybe it's just that I'm an angry young man in a boring, safe job, desperate for a rumble - maybe it's cos I wasn't breast fed as a baby - who fucking knows - but I was ready for the E1 Word Warriors blitzkrieg of SW3 - if we were going down in flames it was gonna be a blaze of glory, if we were going down, we were going down fighting, and hopefully taking a few out with us. That's the way we played it.

Gene confidingly wrapped his arm around my shoulder and drew me close - he smelt good, male, expensive, sweaty - he pushed a brown paper bag into my belly, saying, "Strap it on baby, we're gonna need all the help we can get".

So I'm in the toilet cubicle, fastening on the shoulder holster. I'm fondling the gun gingerly. It's snub nosed - one of those with the revolving cylinder. It has an enamelled badge set in the wooden grip with the word 'Llama'. Gene says it's not a real gun, just a replica. He says there's no firing pin, or something, but it sure as hell looks real to me. The weight! It sure as hell feels mighty real.

Gene wants a change in our act, he wants me to spin the chamber and put the muzzle up against my temple and actually pull the trigger, then I'm to smile psychotically and spin the chamber again, but before I get a second chance he's gonna knock the gun out of my hand. It all sounds great, nice and dramatic, but for some reason I have to look; release the chamber to have a good see if it's empty of ammo, and then, just to be doubly sure, I screw up my face and pull the trigger. The hammer hits with such a force I jump. Replica? All that's missing as far as I can see are the bullets.

As I leave the loo I realise I've got a hard-on, there's something so sexy about having a rod. It's all so fantastically fetishistic. It's about as far away from the normal poetry performance as you can get. Our whole act teeters on the edge - all the best performance teeters on the edge. Fuck knows what people think. Before the piece's appearance they must be faintly (or hopefully *glaringly*) wondering who are these schizoids, high on their own narcissism and bullshit bravura? Then **BANG**, the gun is out and in their faces.

All questions and doubts on our mental make-up are subsidiary. Only three questions remain: Is the gun real? Is it loaded? And, will they use it? When eventually the shooter hits the floor, and the show continues, there is a palpable relaxing of the punters and sighs of relief all round. Brown trousers get sent to the laundry, and everyone can laugh about it later to their friends, - but I have a feeling (and hope) that the lingering doubt remains...

My dad, who was in the war, always used to tell me not to point my toy guns at people (he'd learnt that in the army), and it's true - there's something not nice about staring down a revolver barrel - loaded or not. It's disgraceful. It's the lowest of the low - cheapskate theatre - hey, it's showbiz. Maybe though, one day it won't be just for show. Who knows how serious he is, but G has often talked - the way he does - how he'll go down in history. He says he'll be famous even if it means killing himself on stage. He says "Think of the headlines. The glory. The posthumous anthology!" It's all bullshit - maybe.

There's something about Gene - maybe it's all the wacky backy, I think that's something to do with it, but then again it's also a convenient smoke screen (pardon the pun) - but behind all the posturing there is always an edge of intensity about him. Every performance filled me with a thrilling fear, the unknown element of instability, the volatile, the explosive - sure, this time the gun wasn't loaded, but I had to click, click, click, to make sure. Fuck, I wished I'd had a wank.

As I leave the loo, Maria is walking out of the Ladies, I'm worrying she's just got to notice the bulge in my pants, but she looks like a Mogadonned rabbit in the beams of the headlight. She looks flustered in slow motion. She turns, the door behind her opens, and there's G. He sees me, wipes his hand across his nostrils, then cracks a broad grin. He sidles up close, presses his hand against my side, where the gun is hanging, and says, "Hey, looks like you're primed for action. Let's go big boy."

His hand slides downwards and brushes my thigh. He leads the way down the corridor and out into the arena. My heart's racing.

Gene's moving quickly. I can hear the Bulgarian bollocks has ended. What little audience they had drawn is dissipating, just a few people staying to natter, away from the consumer corridors between the stalls. When we get hard up to the stage the wind chimes are being lifted down the stairs - the stage is empty save for two mikes and boon stands.

A middle class prick in a tuxedo walks up onto the platform, picks up the mike, and in a buck-toothed ee-aw announces there is to be a fifteen minute break before a Flamenco group arrive. The G man mounts the stairs, he walks right up to the prat in the penguin suit, whispers something in his ear, then takes the microphone off him. The bloke looks completely astonished, and has probably never been treated with such discourtesy, but Gene looks very earnest and slightly unsafe, so the MC huffs and puffs, all in a fluster of indignation, but backs away.

G looks brilliantly deranged as he launches into a rant about East End ass kick poetry, declaring that Chelsea's about to witness the rebirth of British verse, via **"The Big City Beats"**. In the immediate vicinity, chattering had stopped, heads were turning. It's time.

Gene's beginning to lose it a little, he needs my support. I run up the stairs and grab the other mike off its stand. We go into performance. Mick Jagger would have been proud. The raised stage gives us the strategic advantage. The Chels set are aghast but intrigued. This is definitely not the usual arts and crafts affair. Some are looking at the pissed-off, retreating MC, others for Security.

Before you could say, "Get the police!" we have scoured their psyches and embedded into their consciousness a few searing words of truth. Well, that's my story. Probably the rich fucks are too addled or sozzled to care, or else too safely ensconced in their middle class cocoons to even give a damn - "Oh such a good idea to get these oiks doing performance poetry, *and* from the East End, wonderful for the Fair yah?"

We're doing beautifully. Our rehearsing's paying off. Not for one moment did we have to wait for the other to do their bit. We were a team. When faced with adversity I absolutely knew I could rely on G, and G absolutely knew he could rely on me. There was a real psychotic edge to our delivery. I'm there, hard into the instant, but I'm also tingling with anticipation of the moment when I will expose the shooter.

It wasn't to be.

It's hard to recollect what exactly happened. The Fair was going on around us. People were buying and selling. Nobody had come to see *us*. What do you do, if you're a Chelsea person, having an evening down at the King's Road Arts Fair, and you come across two aggressive performance poets thrusting their earnest and angst-ridden views of life down on you? Well, if you're cool (and it seemed most of the people attending this event considered themselves to be exceedingly cool), you acknowledge what's going on, but you sure as hell don't show too much empathy, and (God forbid), you certainly don't go giving rapturous support to these oik upstarts - "I mean dahrling, what would everyone think, yah?"

A few of the younger, braver element had collected close to the stage, but they hardly designated what you would call a crowd - their overall reaction seemed to be one of wry amusement, and inquisitiveness as to what we were going to do next. I was too embroiled in remembering the set, to really recognise Gene's responses. I think I did pick up that he was getting irate - but I'd come to expect that. Then it all happened so fast...

We were doing a number called "How Low Can You Go?" where the question is asked (and constantly reiterated), "What is your price?" - the basic assumption being that everyone has a price, no matter who they are or how rich - it's just negotiating how much. G has just stated that he's gonna start the bidding to see what different people's figure is. I shout to the audience, "Well, what if we offered you a thousand pounds?" and so on, until we're asking "Five million pounds?", "Ten million pounds?"

There's one big blond-haired public school prat, right in front of the stage, who keeps on shaking his head. Suddenly the G falls to his knees (he's literally right on top of this guy), he pulls out his wallet, takes out a twenty pound note, and waves it in this Hooray's face, whose expression changes from pantomime scorn to serious hatred. I hear a commotion and look across to see the jilted MC approaching with a burly security guard at his side.

I see a flickering flame in the corner of my vision. Gene has got his lighter out and is attempting to ignite the note.

I hear a yell, and there's a doddery old Chelsea pensioner in full scarlet tunic and chest full of medals, shaking his fist and moving toward the base of the stairs.

I hear a thud, turning in time to catch Gene's head hitting the boards, and to see the Hooray waving the blazing twenty wildly. The Boer War veteran is half way up the stairs, yelling something about treason, closely followed by the security guard.

I make a step toward my compadre who is bleeding from the corner of his mouth, and looking groggy. I fall on one knee to try and help, when G twists round and does a horizontal kick straight to the side of the head of his assailant, who drops like a shot bull - still clutching his charred money. The security guard has passed the scarlet-tunicked grandad, he's removing a big 1rubber torch from his belt clip, when I hear Gene scream, **'Shoot the fucker!'**

The security guard stops in his tracks, only to be bumped into by the Chelsea pensioner, who looks like he's gonna croak from all the exertion. Then Gene's at my side, and he's fumbling inside my jacket, trying to get a grip on the rod. The security guard has half turned to catch the wheezing pensioner. Gene has got a hold on the gun's handle. I grab his hand, and scream, ***"Get the fuck outta here."***

I wrench him by the wrist, and pull him toward the back of the platform. He turns and yells "Maria! Maria!"

I catch a glimpse of her, stood down in the shocked crowd. People turn their heads to see who G's shouting at - she doesn't flinch - just stares straight ahead. We leap down into the stalls - we run.

Eight

I was suffering, waiting for some contact from Gene. Nothing too odd about that, I could tell myself. Gene had gone incommunicado many times before, always to resurface at some point. However, this time it had been a whole month since I'd last seen him.

There was a rumour he'd gone to America. Another, that he was in Sicily with Maria doing some business negotiations. Some drunk down Murphy's said he'd OD'd on some peculiarly strong smack. Gene liked to be talked about - hell he'd probably started the rumours himself. I wasn't really listening - I somehow knew he was alright. I suspected he was probably taking a holiday in Brighton. He was always going on about Brighton, saying it was a young and funky town. He remembered it as a student, when he'd had some wild, romantic love affair. Funny that, cos at some time or another he'd told me he had been a student in Leeds, Manchester, Paris, Edinburgh - Fuck, sure must have some degrees huh?

Nothing exciting happens when Gene is gone.

Where is he? There is only one place to find out. Grove Dwellings. I decide to start with Rhys. I hadn't seen him since the Gurkha knife episode. He's mad. Sure. I must be mad. I walk up the worn concrete steps to his top floor flat.

Rhys, I said I'd tell you about him sometime... Well I guess this is as good a time as any.

Rhys was inhabiting some twilight zone of human existence, living a fine line between being an interesting character and a total crazy. Slightly deranged, yes that's it. For some reason I'm incapable of discriminating between that fine line when the slightly deranged start to become totally unhinged, but I'll keep trying.

I actually found Rhys quite amusing, with his anecdotes about surviving in London. Rhys wasn't a Londoner, he was like the rest of us not even from the East End. He was a Taff from Cardiff, almost public school. He had a strange upbringing, but don't we all? Maybe his upbringing was somewhat stranger than most. His father worked part-time in a health-cum-sex shop in Caroline Street, Cardiff; you know the shop that's a cross between prosthetics and vibrators. Rhys' old man was a big guy who lived a solitary life in a ramshackle farm in mid-Wales which doubled up as a gun club. Rhys' father was heavily into guns. He wanted his ashes put into a container and placed behind the bull's-eye of the target on the gun range. Why do gun clubs attract crazy types? Stupid question really.

The gun - an interesting invention. The power to kill contained in an object you can carry, without getting your hands dirty. The power to kill at a distance. A kind of power that appeals to many men. I'd once asked Rhys if he could get bullets. He asked me the make of the gun.

"Llama," I'd said.

"Oh, Spanish. You'd need 32 calibre S. & W. long. A bit difficult - but, yeh, no problem."

Anyway to top all of this other madness, Rhys' father told him that he was conceived by raping his mother. I don't know about you (and maybe Rhys was telling me porkies) but if you were told something like that by your dad then it could really fuck you up.

Rhys' mother had died when he was twelve and consequently he had doted on her. He'd been raised by his elder sister and an aunt, and it was only when Rhys was sectioned the first time that he saw his father again. To Rhys his father was the law. It was always "father" never "dad". Maybe that was a class thing? Rhys always had a high opinion of himself. I remember when Rhys was on the old King Cole and I suggested he got a job as a postman as there were some vacancies in Whitechapel. He dismissed it with a "I don't do that sort of work." To Rhys this was beneath him.

Of course Rhys took drugs before he went barmy, but since his first incarceration the NHS had deemed it safer for him, safer for everyone, that he remained on high doses of phenothiazines, a major tranquilliser, that quietened the voices, and theoretically enabled him to live in society. Rhys was rather proud of the fact that he had never touched heroin. Sure there were those who did and wore a kind of badge of courage, but then there was the other sort, like Rhys, drugged up to the eyeballs in order to just be able to cope with life, who could (and did) consider themselves somehow superior to the addicts who had to maintain their habits to the class A's by whatever means necessary. There was a definite skewed type of snobbery in some drug circles. There would be people out of their heads on whiz, yapping all sorts of bollocks and giggling at their own rubbish. Show them even a weekend social smackie and they'd curse them for being a junkie.

Double standards, life seems to be full of them. Take Rhys, he thought he was extremely charming with women. You know the type, chocolates, flowers, and he hadn't even kissed them. They'd politely accept his flowers & chocolates, but never go out on a date - they could sense that Rhys was not all there. I have a vivid memory of once seeing him coming down the Cambridge Heath

Road, passing Paul's Records with a bunch of blazing pink gladioli. Waltzing past the trash and litter like some svelte 50's screen idol holding his gladioli like an Oscar. Anyone else would have got a kicking but Rhys had this weird aura around him like some kind of invisible shield. He was completely oblivious to the peculiarity of his situation to the extent that it magically kept him out of harm's way.

Fuck knows what Rhys thought (God preserve us from such a revelation), he'd buy his charming flowers and chocolates, give them to some girl who wouldn't even return his calls, then he'd go spend a fortune on hookers. Double standards sure - I've got plenty of my own.

I arrive on the top landing and I'm outside Rhys' door. I don't really want to see Rhys, especially after last time, I mean it's almost always more trouble than it's worth. I can justify it however, I want to find out the whereabouts of Gene. However.... However, I also really want to see if Rhys has gotten worse. Am I sick?

I knock lightly, and coo Rhys' name. His front door opens and I am greeted with a cheeky grin. Rhys is dressed in a silk paisley dressing gown. "Spike, I'm watching a great video - come in, come in."

I forgot to mention Rhys was also into hard porn, he thought it was terribly amusing. His dealer of dirty videos was, in fact, his local corner shop; a newsagents-cum-grocers-cum-video shop - you know the kind, and his supplier was an Indian lady in her mid thirties, complete with sari and kids and husband and... well it seemed bizarre to me.

I walk in and there is the TV in the corner of the room, with an image of a black woman having a coke bottle inserted into her rectum. To tell the truth I'm quite shocked. Rhys is very up - he gets that way sometimes - I will have to play along for a while before I can ask the questions I need.

"Just checking to see the film isn't damaged. I could not believe it Spike, recently my luck has been getting worse. Picture this, there I am jacking off the old hammer to this brilliant German porn. Did I tell you that German porn is the best? Anyway what happens?"

"What?"

"The video only gets stuck."

"Stuck?"

"Yeh no freeze frame but stuck in the fucking machine, so I don't get my jollies and I'm over my time limit at the shop. So not only do I have to explain it to Mrs Ghandi but I've got to get some technical geezer to unfix the video."

"Sounds funny to me."

"Well I wasn't laughing Spike, I had to pay this electrician and you know what, he asked if he could watch the video all the way through."

"Cheeky."

"You're damn right, cheeky bastard. Couldn't have him prying now, could I?"

I shake my head in order to look like I agree. It's all feeling somewhat strange.

"I don't know Spike, you can't trust anyone these days. Everyone is on the take. Thirty pounds can you believe it! Never mind I'm coming into money soon, I can feel it in my bones."

"Your bones?"

"It's a saying Spike. Sometimes I'm astounded by how naïve you are."

"Me?"

"Yes you. Really Spike, you can be so ridiculously stupid sometimes."

"Fuck off" I say.

"Ooh really. Language Spike, language! You should watch what you say when there's a lady present."

"What the...?"

Rhys puts his finger to his lips and points over to the easy chair in front of the TV. There sat a blow up doll fully clothed in a red dress. Her vacant expression and open mouth made her look like she was in a state of permanent shock.

"What...."

"You mean who. That's Candy. She's great, she doesn't grouse, gripe and..." Rhys leans over to me and affectedly, behind the back of his hand whispers, "Don't tell anyone but she's great in bed."

Rhys has gotten worse. But I am fascinated. I'm intrigued and a little bemused that the mere talking of Candy seemed to imbue her with life. It was no longer Rhys and me but Candy too.

"Don't worry Rhys, your secret is safe with me."

I get a very strong feeling that I ought to just ask for any information on the whereabouts of Gene, make my excuses and go. I say nothing. I stay.

"You're shocked."

"Me? No, it's just where did you meet her?" I am saying stupid things. I cannot stop myself.

"Funny you should ask but I think it was fate." Rhys cocks his head to one side and gets a wan, faraway look.

"Tell me more" I say (I don't know why, I really don't).

"Well, I was in Soho and thought I'd check out the sex shops, you know, see what videos were on offer, and I was just looking at a row of blow up dolls, hanging there in their packets. There were all different types, it's fascinating!"

I nod in agreement.

"Then, for no apparent reason one fell from its hook and landed at my feet. Of course I could have ignored it... but Spike, this was the weird thing... I knew Candy had done what she did because.... Because she'd been waiting for me."

"Really?"

"Yes, really. With my track record with women? Definitely. Hey yours isn't any better, you should get one. Yeh it would be great, we could have tea, me, you, Candy and... and Edie."

"Edie?"

"Yes Spike, Edie, it's a good name. The girls can talk while we retire to the conservatory to smoke our cigars. It'll be great."

I really feel I should diffuse this insanity by stating "Rhys, blow up dolls don't talk, you've got no conservatory, I don't smoke and **you're totally fuckin' demented!**" Instead I nod, as if in agreement.

"Tea?"

I stare vaguely at Rhys, then turn my head and look at the doll in her skimpy dress and gobsmacked expression, then finally at the video, where a child is having her arms broken with a claw hammer by a man in a leather mask, while a black woman is fucking her with a strap-on dildo.

"You know your trouble Spike?"

"No?"

"You've got no imagination and you call yourself a poet? You just don't get it do you? You'll never get it."

I turn to see Rhys holding Candy's hand. She

sports a diamond ring. Caressing her arm Rhys looks at her, then me and there's a tear in his eye. "Candy is the best girl I could ever have, no one could hold a candle to her."

"If they did she'd blow up." I don't know why I said that. Rhys looks distressed - angry.

"Anyone hurts Candy and they'll have to deal with me. No one hurts Candy. Am I making myself clear?"

"Crystal clear." The atmosphere is getting edgy. "I must go Rhys."

"Not before you kiss Candy."

"What?"

"Kiss Candy. She wants a goodbye kiss."

"Rhys?"

"Kiss."

Like a sleep walker I approach Rhys and Candy. I bend down, peck her on the cheek.

"Not good enough Spike, on the mouth, and no tongue."

I'm looking at Candy, but I can feel Rhys' eyes boring into my cranium. I kiss Candy full on the mouth.

'Good Spike, very good. Candy likes you, I can see that I'll have to watch you in future.'

"Hey Rhys..." I can't think of anything to finish this sentence. "Look I must go."

I fumble with the door handle and stumble out of the flat with the smell of vinyl in my nostrils. My senses are blurred. I don't think I can handle this. Rhys has lost it, and I'm not all that sure about me.

Was there some point, when it went, or was it just always going, slipping imperceptibly? Maybe we're all losing ourselves in one way or another. Being responsible and consistent and adult is so hard. We cling to our existence like climbers to the rock face. We use all our effort to hold on to stability, safety - but we hang precariously. It doesn't require much effort to just turn around - a moment - a moment is all it takes to just turn around and... step off - to just... let yourself go. It is of course harder to get back once gone. I was living in that twilight world; betwixt, between... not sure of which way to turn. I needed to find Gene. I *had* to find him *now*.

Stop me any day of the week and I'd probably be waiting for some contact from Gene. Like the ever hopeful Jehovah posse waiting for the second coming, I'm waiting. Look I'm not comparing G to Christ here though... It's more like the old Velvet's song, 'Waiting For The Man'. I want my fix. It's not the man I want, I want what he's got to give me... No. I dunno! OK, G probably couldn't have given a fuck about me. That's his scene. Maybe not? Maybe that's why I'm writing this; to find out why we happened at all - to find out more about myself or more about G - to find out what the fuck exactly did happen...

Maria was now in the frame. It was no worry; I'd seen this many times before. For G, people came and went. He had lots of acquaintances, not many friends. Lots of people thought they knew him. Lots of people seemed to have a story to tell about G. Maybe I'm just one of those people. Maybe this is my story. Me and him were close yet far apart.

Do people genuinely fall in love? I don't think so. They just provide a need for each other, and there's real comfort in being needed; it can make for a good reason to persevere with life.

"Ooh baby, do you love me, really, really

love me?"

"Yes, of course I do."

"Well say it, go on say it."

Bollocks! People are fucked as far as I can see. They invent lots of rules, codes of conduct, social mores, religious rituals, therapies, clubs, cliques - trying to fill the vacuum, trying to fill the hole. Trying to avoid the real issues, trying to avoid asking the real question. Fuck, at least Gene never lied to me - he never told me he loved me - he never even told me he needed me.

I know what you're thinking, "Why doesn't he drop this asshole and get on with his own life? Why doesn't he jettison this G character, he sounds dodgy, unreliable, a waste of emotional investment." Maybe that's what you're thinking. Maybe not. All I know is no man or woman is an island. Sure we all need our space, but haven't you been in a team, group, relationship, and felt stronger, felt less alone? Suddenly you seem to have an objective. Relationships can be a lot of hard work, but in a relationship you feel needed, there's a sense of purpose, you've got direction. Yeah I know it's difficult to know if you're on course, and exactly where you're going, and many's the time you'll be thinking, "Who is running this show?" As I see, in relationships people are so insecure that they need to be reassured all the time. Relationships are fucked as far as I can see. Fucked, but necessary.

G and me? What a pair! I doubt if either of us were good for each other. It could be masochism or pure hedonism - all I know is that G seemed right for me at the time, and I obviously suited him. Life is too short. Too many opportunities are missed. We had to take our chance. Take it to the limit - to oblivion. Maybe that's what we wanted.

We can spend all our lives running away from ourselves. Me? Sure, I was on the run; running on empty, running up the down escalator, running at the mouth, running out of ideas, running away from my life, myself. Running, running... Running to somewhere, nowhere, anywhere. Running towards an end, whatever that may be. The thing is to keep running. Stop and... and then what? Me and G kept running...

Nine

..................We ran out of the Chelsea Town Hall chaos. My heart was pumping quick time. Nobody had tried to confront us, as we scrambled through the aisles of stalls. I found a fire exit at the back of the hall and when we burst out into daylight, as if by some miracle, there was G's white Vauxhall. We piled in.

"Come on, just go!" I shouted.

"No Spike, it's OK - everything's OK. You're OK." Gene was calm. Unnervingly calm.

"What the fuck? It's not fucking OK. Fucking well drive."

"No Spike, I'm gonna wait for Maria."

"What?" I exclaimed.

"I said I'm gonna wait for Maria."

"**Fucking arsehole!**" I yelled.

I got out of the motor, and slammed the door. I began walking south, in the direction of the Embankment. I didn't know what I was going to do, but I was too scared to be seen on the Kings Road. I just wanted to be as far away from the potential repercussions as possible. I'd only got about 50 yards when the real terror set in. I heard the *whah, whah* of a police siren, and began to get really fearful, thinking here I was on foot, dressed in a black wool suit on a balmy summer evening. I was imagining that the hooray Henry was probably comatosed, the Chelsea pensioner ~~probably~~ suffering from a stroke, a warrant out for my arrest, an APB with my description. *

My heart was beating double-quick time. I think about taking off my jacket, I thought somehow it would be less easy to identify me, but then I remembered the gun. The gun! How the fuck did I ever forget? I wanted to run, but I'm thinking it's gonna look too suspicious.

in the holster, strapped across my shoulder.

I walk quickly, I'm pissing sweat. I'm on Cheyne Walk, I see a boozer. I'm thinking I'll go in and ring a cab - I've got to get off the street - when I hear a *beep*, *beep*, *beep*. I turn, ready to flee, ready to surrender, and there's G. He's smiling and waving. Maria's at his side, she's laughing. They pull up abreast of me. Maria opens the back door. I get in.

"Oh, youz looka zo funny Meester Spike Man."

I probably did, but I certainly don't feel like laughing. I lie down on the back seat, partially out of fatigue, partly out of fear of being seen.

"Take me home," I moan.

G and Maria are laughing.

"Ha, fucking ha," I bemoan. "Were in deep now. They'll know how to find us. They will."

"How comes Spikey babe?"

"The guy that got us the gig."

"What guy? Nobody got us the gig. Nobody invited us. I just wanted to do something in Chelsea. I like Chelsea."

This was confusing, but I let it seep in.

"Hey soldier, you look like you're suffering battle fatigue - chill out my man. Relax."

"Fuck." I say.

Maria turns around in her seat, she's got a smile on her face, but when she sees how distraught I must have looked, she changes her look to empathy and compassion. I remember that look; the earlier distance and aloofness were a vague memory, when I saw the genuine concern on her face I wanted to dive into her being; she was mother, lover, sister, friend. I wanted her to cuddle me, take me home, instead she reached into her patent leather clutch bag and proffered me a red capsule.

"Eetsa OK. Take-a the pill. Don'ta worry."

She was a nurse, a sister of mercy, she had nothing but my best interest and welfare at heart. I loved her. I swallowed the capsule.

Gene's spirits are very high. He's been fired up by the madness of the evening, and he talks at me, looking at me in the rear view. He's using fighting talk. I don't reply, just slide back down onto the seat, watch the sky going by, and G's words are just flack passing overhead, as I hide in the secure bunker of forgetfulness.

The street lamps are coming on, and a warm dark blanket of night enfolds me. A new Prince song is playing on the car cassette and G's raving on about the lyrics. I vaguely hear something about *"But if a night falls// And a bomb falls// Will anybody see the dawn?// Time// Time."* The stars are coming out down the Embankment. I'm a little person in a great big galaxy. Nothing matters. Nothing matters.

Ten

I did not dream.

I wake up in my own bed. I feel like I've been lobotomised. Then slowly I begin remembering. I'm back home. Back from the Chelsea chaos. Back to the safety of the familiar war zone of E1. West End to fag end. What's going on? This is my life? I live here? God I feel like an alien! Any aliens reading this, where the fuck are you? I'm ready. What about Gene? Maybe he's an alien? *Don't be stupid Spike.*

Listen, we're all little people on a small planet in a big galaxy that is in itself tiny in the greater universe, but if you've got a dream to hold on to, it's *your* dream, it's a *big* dream. What's your dream? What are you doing? Everyone has their reasons. Some of us don't want to face them. Some of us want to erase them. "There are actions and there are consequences" - G was always saying that. G usually made the actions and left everyone else with the consequences. But maybe I'm shirking my responsibilities here. It was becoming my motto.

Eleven

It's over 10 years since the Arts Fair gig. I'm thirty-nine now. Ten years older. I'm a house owner, a long term partner, fuck, a father. The world would say I'm doing OK. Instead I'm in pain. I'm grieving. I had a taster of some other kind of existing, some more exciting way. But I didn't, I wouldn't take responsibility. Do I sound pathetic? I guess I am. There, I've said it. That's the kind of thing I'd never tell nobody - never. Hey, maybe you should try it sometime. It won't change your life, but a little humility is hard to find these days. Fuck! Fuck, Fuck, Fuck! Me and the G? Of course it was frustrating, annoying, sometimes just damn stupid. How much of what eventually happened was my responsibility? I had a good keen sense of self preservation. Aw, how can I put it? I would not walk into hell, or put myself in the line of fire, to die for Gene... but, writing this I'm so unsure... I know I'm still angry. I know I'm still doubtful of this, and many other questions... I'm angry with myself. Who knows what I would have done... Damn him. Double damn him. Some people get under your skin like the junkie's hypo - ~~giving~~ supplying the life giving/life taking elixir... Necessary. Yes, that's what G was to me then... He was necessary.

* Either remove completely or else rewrite

Twelve

I shouldn't really be so hard on myself. Things always look different in hindsight, don't they? I used to know a girlfriend, Julie was her name, and she always read the end of a book before reading the start. I thought this was odd, but she said it gave her more objectivity and a better perspective on the book. I mean we all die and that's a fact, but death doesn't give anyone a new insight into their life. Having not died yet, my comments are open to argument. Perhaps we see all on our deathbed, a bit of a bugger that, I mean a little insight in mid-life would not go amiss.

Julie? She was ambitious, independent, she was great in bed, she was going places... without me. I'd met her in Cardiff; my first big love. At the time she was on a journalism course. Julie had decided her future - I hadn't any idea what I was going to do. She was determined to become a young thrusting reporter, eager to make her mark in the media. She got her first break as a court reporter on the West Briton. Blinded by first-love dreams I followed her to Cornwall. I would have done anything for her. She progressed in her chosen career, I ended up stacking tins of beans in Tescos. Of course it all fell apart....

If you are reading this Julie I'd just like to say I'm not bitter. It's all part of the discordant melody we call life. Sometimes you meet somebody and you think you've found the lost chord, singing a love song duet in perfect harmony, then the needle jumps and wham, she's high in the charts, and you're back in the bargain basement. Wonder where Julie is these days? Shit happens. Gene was always saying that.

Thirteen

I took Clare to The Passage To India, it was our anniversary. I'm not exactly sure what that particular date meant, in so much as I can't remember if it was when we actually first met, or if she was judging it from when we consummated the affair (there was only a couple of weeks difference anyway, so it doesn't really matter, does it? I let Clare remember stuff like that) - fuck knows. I'd gotten pissed and asked her to marry me - we had some good sex that night. Next morning she was really sweet and I didn't have the heart to tell her I'd only said it cos I was drunk. So I bought her a ring - it cost a fortune. We haven't fixed a date for the wedding. It's all a bit much really.

Our one year anniversary. I thought The Passage To India, Mile End Road, was a good idea; it's very pleasant, the waiters are very respectful, the decor is nice, you know flock wallpaper like what the Indians like and tapestried chairs, tasteful, plants - it's also, for the quality of food and service, unbelievably cheap.

Well, we'd only just settled ourselves in - Clare is deciding what we are going to eat - when I hear, "Mr.Campbell - oh yes - good to see you mate - oh yes - very good," and there's the maître d' beaming from ear to ear hugging Gene. Yes Gene and Maria. They're all dressed up. Gene's got a black silk jacket with one of those sticky-up Chinese type collars, Maria's wearing a little strappy black dress and a lovely pair of gold sandals - which hardly seem to be sandals at all - just thin golden threads holding the soles together. The maître d' seems overwhelmed that such glamorous clientele are gracing his humble establishment. It was wonderfully touching to watch...

"Spike," Gene comes towards me. I half rise. He shakes my hand. "Hello..." he says to Clare - an almost imperceptible pause.

"Clare," I exclaim, "this is Maria."

"Ah zo, itza good eh, I ere zo much about you." Which I know cannot be true, but Clare casts a little appreciative glance towards me.

So here's Gene and Maria, stood side by side at our table. The maître d' is fussing about apologetically saying something about he didn't realise. A waiter arrives and starts laying extra places.

"No no mate, here please, yes." The maître d' is shaking his head and holding the waiter's arm. "Here please. Yes, yes, alright?"

He gestures towards the front of the restaurant, "Nice table here, oh yes very nice."

He's lithely pulled out Clare's chair. He's ushering us over to a table in the window.

So there we are the four of us exchanging banter. There are two waiters gracefully bumbling around arranging our table. It all feels very special. I'm very glad this has happened, it's saved me from having to struggle through an evening of stilted conversation with Clare (who has just put her hand on my thigh for an instant). Gene will no doubt entertain us; the way Gene does.

But it's different. Gene is not being his usual up-tempo self. He's sitting there answering when asked, but not engaging in or promoting conversation. Marie and Clare seem to have hit it off; they're giggling a bit, heads close, probably talking about make-up or something.

The waiter brings our starters. I'm looking at Gene. The waiter half bows deferentially. Gene says "thank you." It seems like the waiter is waiting for something - or maybe it's me who's waiting - waiting for Gene to be Gene.

I sit; opposite Gene, diagonal to Maria, next to Clare. I can't help watching the way Maria throws her head when she laughs - I like to watch, there's something salacious, inviting about the way she moves. When she's finished her starter she unashamedly takes out a compact, powders her nose, applies deep red lipstick; she's so erotic, womanly. I cast a glance at Clare; she's so plain, so unassuming. I look back to Maria - I cannot stop looking - the way her breasts heave, the cleavage a dark inviting 'y'. I'm sat there feeling a sexy dark warm with half a hard-on. I get a bit self-conscious.

Gene's a lucky man. I hate the confidence of his relationship; there's Maria exuding come-on sexuality, there's Gene looking glum.

Clare puts her hand on my thigh again and slides it affectionately towards my crotch. She feels the lump in my pants, presses it furtively, coquetishly flutters her eyes towards me, a wispish grin across her lips. I smile back.

Then, without any forewarning, Maria rises. She pushes down her dress; both hands moving elegantly, sliding from her waist to her thigh - it's inviting – it's like she's enjoying touching herself – it's like she's foreplaying with herself, and inviting us all to watch. I'm self-conscious as I gape; I can't stop myself. I'm worried Clare's just got to notice, but I have to stare, this is like a limited offer, I don't know if I'm ever going to get the opportunity again. Clare squeezes my growing bulge.

"Where ze bathroom - eh?" says Maria and blurts a little embarrassed giggle – it's so endearing. I just sit, taking it all in; her petite figure, perfect proportions, her hair, her neck, breasts, stomach, her olive arms, bare legs, everything. She glances at me. She likes it. I look to Gene who's just staring into space...

Clare stumbles up, "I'll come too. It's this way," and she points to the stairs. I'm sure Clare has noticed my gawking - I kind of don't care - I wish Clare would take some pointers from Maria - she must know this is what I like.

I watch as Maria slinks her way down the room. I wish I could watch as she wiggles up the stairs, but I can't see properly from where we are.

The girls are gone. I look at Gene, raise my eyebrows, smile stupidly.

"Ray's dead."

"Pardon?"

"Raymond Carver died last week, and you know Spike, nobody told me."

I did not know then that Raymond Carver was a famous poet. I assumed it must be a friend of G's. Gene's looking at me like he wants some sort of an answer, I actually thought at that moment that he was going to cry, so I look at him and make a face trying to look like I'm sympathetic.

"Time's a great healer," I say - cos it's all I could think to say.

Gene looks at me in a non-committal, blank

way, and I wished I could have been more convincing. I'm crap at situations like this. Gene made me feel even worse when he says "Yeah", without the vaguest trace of optimism or hope. I'm wishing the girls would return or the waiter would interrupt or the fucking floor would open up and swallow me. Gene has both hands flat on the table - he's like a man in shock, steadying himself. His face expressionless, yet sad. He's looking straight at me, but I don't think he's seeing anything.

"Dead," he whispers, "Dead," and he shakes his head.

It is unsettling seeing my friend locked inside his own grief. I feel awkward, useless. I don't know what to do. I feel a massive pressure; it's as if the room is breathing in on me. I want to get up, run, but I am glued to my seat. I seem to be trapped in a dense treacle of the moment. Time and motion are dulled to near stationary. I slowly turn my head away from Gene. I look around at all the diners, and realise that everyone in this restaurant, every one of us will die. All of us. I feel an intense sadness. I catch the waiter's eye, and am saved from my thoughts. Immediately he is at our table. "Ah yes sir?"

"A pint of lager please?"

The waiter turns towards Gene... then just backs away.

Death. We're just not very well adapted to death in this country are we? We see it on the news, hear about it all the time. It's an important feature in movies – we like a bit of death don't we? (If I was going to write a book I'd have some death in it). But we don't actually see it – not really – not real death. Somehow we're hidden from real death. To tell the truth I like it that way. To tell the truth I don't want to think about death...

Ah here's the girls!

Well, well, Clare looks different – more... radiant?... And Maria! As I stare I notice other male heads turn and also stare, we can't help ourselves. Maria is like a magnet for men's eyes – she looks so confidently *SEXY*.

"Ah the girls!" I say aloud as they approach.

Gene removes his hands from the table-top and makes an attempt to stop looking so fucking depressing.

Maria stands (for a tiny moment longer than necessary) then shimmies down onto her chair – smiles and pouts. Clare does a stupid parody of the same and giggles self-consciously. Clare's eyes seem ablaze with knowledge and bravado, which is most unusual. There's some strange stupid secret that the women share – Lord knows what they've been doing in the ladies room!

So there I am with the girls being all girlie and there I am with Gene being all glum...

And there I am.

I don't really know what to do; Gene is there in body, but his spirit has vacated the soiree. I just want to gawp at Maria. I haven't got a clue how to speak to her. Right now she's smoking.

Then the strangest thing happens. Clare starts talking. She's going on about performance poetry. This is weird. I didn't realise Clare knew anything about the subject. Right now she's telling

Maria about John Cooper Clarke, how he used to be so unmitigatingly strong, performing in between punk bands, dodging cans and spit, giving the world street-tough poetry. How he could have changed the face of modern performance poetry, and instead changed into a cardboard cut-out parody of himself, doing silly ditties and daft jokes for student unions. She sounds very knowledgeable and decidedly passionate. I am amazed. I look at her open-mouthed.

"Isn't that right?" she says.

I nod, not really cos I agreed, but just that Clare was being so opinionated and dogmatic, it was completely out of character. Maria looked absolutely enthralled. I was taken aback, but also awe-struck to see Clare raving on in this manner. I'm using the opportunity to look some more at Maria, whose completely engaged in Clare's tirade. Maria keeps "Uh, huhing" and "Ah zo-ing", putting her hand to her face, polished fingernails gracing her skin, then on her breast, her belly. She gasps, little gasps, like faint cries, like erotic foreplay moans, her breast heaving, her eyes widening.

We've all been ignoring Gene. Suddenly he stands up.

"I'm going," he states.

And nobody says anything. And we're all looking at Gene. And there's a waiter at Gene's side. And then there's the maître d' and he's worriedly asking Gene if everything's alright and Maria's answering for Gene, "Eetza OK, he hear his friend dead. Eetza OK. Eetza OK yes?"

And Maria's stood up. And the maître d' looks at me, and I shrug my shoulders and gesticulate with my palms up.

And Clare's stood up. And Maria is holding her clutch bag and she reaches across the table and hugs Clare and kisses her cheek. And the waiter's got the bill on a plate. And Gene doesn't even look at it; he reaches in his wallet and pulls out four twenties and puts them on the plate. And there they are walking towards the front door. And the maître d' flits past them and fumbles for the handle.

And there is a poignant moment. Gene has raised his hand to his face and the maître d' has extended his hand towards Gene's face. And they clasp hands in the overarm position (like some gentle arm wrestlers) and they hold it, just for the briefest moment. Then Gene is through the door. And I watch the little black dress and petite figure, and the bare legs and the sandals that are hardly sandals at all, and her bottom and trim waist. I'm glad I can watch. And they are gone.

Clare and I finish our meal. And the waiters are wonderfully subservient and the maître d' has a deferential maître d'-type chat with us, and says we must give Mr.Campbell his deepest sympathies. Clare is sat there with Maria's lipstick on her cheek and I do not tell her. I wondered - still do - how Clare could talk so passionately, so knowledgeably about the birth of British performance poetry. The only person I had ever heard talk like that was Gene. What has been going on?

When we got back to her place, I grabbed her as soon as the front door shut. And I've got her against the hall wall and I'm kissing her face; my lips against the lipstick trace. And Clare's got her eyes closed and I close mine. And I'm ripping open her blouse and she's groaning. And I'm pulling up her skirt and she's moaning. And I've gotten my hand inside her knickers and she's squealing, sighing, gasping. My middle finger is up inside her. She's so wet, so wet. And there we were. My pants around my ankles, and my hands around her arse cheeks, her legs wrapped around my thighs. And I'm thudding her into the wall and she's squeezing me in her scissor lock. And we're both crying and groaning. And I open my eyes just before I come, and she's coming too, and her eyes open briefly. And I shut my eyes cos there is Clare, the most orgasmic, passionate I have ever seen her, she's shouting, "Yes. Yes!" And as I come, it's Maria I'm thinking of. It's Maria!

Fourteen

I dunno. Are we merely at the vagaries of forces outside our control?

As a child I always thought that things would get easier when I became a man. Now I know I was wrong, it just gets harder. It reminds me of a line Bill Burroughs wrote to Jack Kerouac, it said: "Because if there is one thing I feel sure of it is this, that Human life has *direction*". Maybe some of us spend half of our lives figuring where did it all go wrong, and how did we get here? Some appear to swagger through life without a care; it's as if they're not trying, certainly not worrying or analysing their existence.

Direction? This poetry thing seemed like some kind of script - plenty of words, but direction? What were we trying to do? The mantra of our times was 'look after number one', but we were two. We wanted to cut through the bullshit of the age we found ourselves in. Fuck it was hard. It was our stab at trying to make something out of our lives. Sure we'd like to cut through the all pervading selfishness, the *Me Generation* philosophies that made real human communication impossible. A to Z in one easy move.

Some people would say, "but toil and trouble makes life more interesting". They're probably the people who have no toil or trouble in their lives - they're probably the intellectual observers of the scene - observers like the guilt-ridden poets we were trying not to become. "Ooh, with its ups and downs life is so-o-o interesting". Well you can take that self-satisfied "interesting" and shove it. Life is all suffering, so the Buddha says, I don't necessarily agree, but he sure has more fans than we do. During one of my many worried moments I remember Gene saying,

"Look, Christ and his disciples weren't hip to the Romans, or the scribes, in fact they were detested, and poor old Jesus got banged up on the cross by them. From small acorns Spike - from small acorns... Now His words are spread across the globe. His readers number millions."

This parallel with the growth of Christianity and our present predicament as the unrecognised London poetry duo The Big City Beats seemed a little off beam. Gene was full of shit a lot of the time.

What ever made me believe this stuff? I wanted to – it's as simple or as complicated as that. When you've got fuck-all to believe in, then anything will do. We were making it up as we went along and then selling ourselves our own ideas. We were like two sleazy car salesmen, with one knackered vehicle between us and no customers. Careering, good word - that's it, we were careering. Tryna make some kind of career. Maybe we were careering out of control. We just carried on.

Neither of us really aired our fears or doubts, we just kept on going; doing gigs nobody wanted us to do, gate crashing where we were not invited, shoving poetry in people's faces.

I remember early on in our brief career, on the way to an audition at Apples & Snakes in Covent Garden, Gene, hyped-up and typically verbose, told me his theory on the subject of being afraid - "Yes Spike there is a fear - but that fear is simply the fear of failure. We got to be careful here Spike, that fear can stop us dead in our tracks, can stop us from attempting to succeed. Yes, it's hard Spike - hard to face up to that fear and see it for what it really is - but we have to Spike, it must be done. We have nothing to fear but fear itself. We *must* face it. We must face it, embrace it and then, and then Spike... we must erase it. Got that Spike? Fear is nothing to be afraid of."

The pep talks were many. Most of the time I felt like saying "Jesus Gene - shut the fuck up." I never did. Those words to me were like the whispered sweet nothings of an insincere lover, part of you knows them for what they are, part of you desperately wants to be told... told anything, believe... anything. Whenever G was with me... I believed.

So we carried on carrying on. Big gigs. Little gigs. Good gigs, crap gigs. Poetry gigs were fairly common, but *good* poetry gigs were as rare as the second coming. It seemed that by its very nature, poetry was not/could not elevate itself from the self imposed mire in which it was stuck; had been stuck for as long as anyone could remember. So poets accepted that gigs were always shambolic, that organisation was to be chaotic, that somehow poetry time ran slower and was more convoluted that real time... Everyone just accepted the situation. Nobody thought they could change it - consequently the people involved in the scene were for the most part eccentric, apathetic, dead beats. It used to upset me, but it made G rage. He wasn't in the poetry game as some pastime or hobby equivalent to am-dram or trainspotting.

We were determined to change things. As

far as Gene was concerned, we were willing to do our bit, so what the fuck was wrong with everyone else? Poets and poetry audiences were not who we were performing for, and yet... *there was nobody else!* Is this madness or what? It seemed the only people who thought we were any good were the kind of people I would not normally want to meet; crazy, fucked-up people.

It was usually left to me to do the talking off stage, Gene chose to be stand-offish. I think he'd learnt somewhere that people are only really interested in a stage persona, and that they don't really want to find out that you're a human being. I think Gene was wrong, but he chose his own path. I think his ideas of real and stage persona got a bit too scrambled. He thought he had to act in public, he thought he had to act when he was with me, and all that happened was he distanced himself more and more. But he maintained a front, he kept inventing and re-inventing a world to inhabit, because he was not exactly enamoured by the one we found ourselves living in.

What kind of world was I living in? I seemed to be inhabiting two worlds. A world of nine to five that saw me in an office, in a suit, and then, more and more my other world centred around E1; more precisely Whitechapel, and very particularly Grove Dwellings.

Grove Dwellings consisted of two low rise late Victorian blocks of yellow London brick with a central courtyard. They had been built in 1898 without bathrooms and the absolute minimum space and amenities for working class people to survive. Now they were squats and home to the Grovers, a mixture of anarchists and bohemians. Grove Dwellings acted as a magnet for misfits and drifters who wanted to live outside of the mainstream. I was drawn towards the Grovers, and the colourful chaos that was their lives. A huge part of their social life focused on the nearest pub; Murphys, a run-down establishment which welcomed them with open arms. You'd find me at Murphy's most weekends.

Fifteen

It's Saturday. There we were outside Murphy's. It was mid afternoon and Shaun the manager had all the doors of the pub open. He'd put white plastic chairs and tables outside with massive banana yellow umbrellas. Shaun walked about with sunglasses on and was wearing an outlandish Hawaiian shirt and the most ludicrous Day-Glo green and yellow Bermuda shorts. The Copacobana comes to Whitechapel - drink al fresco and die of carbon monoxide poisoning - yeah!

There we were. Gene was sipping a mineral water with ice and lemon, he had decided that alcohol fucked your brain and he needed to think straight. I was impressed with his resolve. Gene was wearing a white T-shirt, white shorts, and a sailor's cap. He was reading intently, reading theatrically (*is that possible?*), anyway I had to ask...

"What's the book Gene?"

"Interesting Spike. Very interesting yer-rh."

"Yer-rh?"

Gene pretends to read some more. I try to ignore him. Probably two minutes elapses, then very deliberately G puts the open book face down on the table. "Yes, it's called *Everything Is Negotiable*, and you know? This guy is right."

"Waddya mean, 'everything'?"

"Everything Spikey, everything. Sex, money, fame, power... everything."

"Everything?"

Gene nodded.

"Yeah? Well what if you've been kidnapped by a psycho who had a gun to your head?"

"You negotiate Spike, ne-gotiate. You

admire the fact that he's in total control - tell him you think he's got pizzazz, guts. You play to his strengths. Then you point out to him that there are bigger, far more profitable people who he could abduct. Tell him that a man of his wherewithal doesn't want to waste his time messing with small fry."

"What if he won't listen?"

"You wait to catch him off guard, nick his gun and blow his brains out."

"That simple," I say sarcastically.

Gene pretends not to notice. He looks out, across The Strip, eyes squinting against the glare – then, without looking at me, he speaks steadily, deliberately. "Like the book says, everything is negotiable – everything..."

I decide to force the situation. "And The Beats – are we negotiable?" I ask.

"Flexibility Spike. Like a reed will bend to the force of the hurricane, while others, less inflexible get shattered into so many fragments." Gene still stares down The Strip, "The Beats are art, but just like any other art that you've ever heard of, it's not as simple as just being good – you've got to be marketed – do negotiations. Andy Warhol understood this. It's a matter of knowing when to compromise, when to stand firm."

Gene's know-it-all guru calm was making my blood boil. Compromise! I feel I've compromised most of my life. Everything had been a fucking compromise from avoiding the school bullies to ending up as a supermarket shelf stacker following some stupid love dream that ended in nothing. My white collar nine to five was a compromise, my engagement to Clare was a compromise, and now Gene wanted The Beats to compromise. Fuck it. Fuck the fucking compromises.

"**Fuck!**" I shout out loud.

Gene does not even move or alter his expression. Nobody walking by turned or said anything.

"Fucking fuck fuck fuck fuck."

I look around, nothing had changed, but I felt better. Sometimes we all need to shout "FUCK". Maybe you should try it. Go on.

So there we were, me and G sat there - catching the last rays of summer and looking down The Strip in silence. Nothing is being said. Nothing has happened for a while. Nothing is planned. I look at Gene in his immaculate matelot outfit, his suntan. I'm sat here with the top button of my shorts undone. I'm twenty nine now, and I am old, I'm fat. The flesh of my belly looks like potato – a creased and puckered, hairy spud. What is going to happen? Where is my life going? I mean my plans didn't even stretch as far as next week, never mind a strategy for life. I was thinking I've had enough compromise. I was always thinking that. But this time I opened my mouth.

"Well if everything is negotiable isn't it time we started some negotiations?"

"Ooh Spike, I love it when you're all manly."

Gene turns to me. He fixes me firmly with those dazzling eyes, his gorgeous smile. "Television, Spike."

"Yes?" I said.

"Yes, Spike."

"Yes, what?" - Jesus who writes these scripts? It's a game. Some game G's devised. A game of catch - and dumb me - I always get caught.

"Spike, imagine, even if we go on Night Network at 4am, we're gonna reach more people than a lifetime of schlepping round the poetry circuit. Video Spike. Video."

What the fuck am I doing? I'm a fucking dupe again - a victim of Gene's marauding mind. Gene's got me playing in his mind games again, and I'm IT! I shouldn't let him play with me like this. I shouldn't.

"What the fuck are you talking about?" I wail.

"Come on Spike, stop messing me around. We're gonna make a video; we're gonna be legends in other people's living rooms. Spike, we're gonna make ourselves TV celebrities. Yey-heh-hey."

Acting. G's always acting - always, always.

I decided it was time to challenge him. "Do you always talk in sound bites? There aren't any cameras. What is this shit?"

Gene shrugs his shoulders, sticks out his bottom lip and responds with "You've got to be in it to win it."

In it - that's where I was - hook, line and sinker - he knew how to draw me in. Yeah, I wanna be a TV star. Yeah of course I do - just like you. Any kinda star, any would do. TV, Movies, Media - I wanna be famous. I wanna be seen in *Hello* magazine with a staple through my navel, waving you goodbye. Is my honesty overwhelming you? I hope so. Yes I'm selfish and self centred and .... aw, I'm a lot of things, just like everyone else. I have been a punk, a rapper, a poet. I've been a brother, a son, a lover, a friend, an enemy, employed, unemployed, abused, abusive, I've been cruel, kind, happy, sad, busy, idle etc., etc. - I am many things, at the same time and at different times. Would you believe me if I told you I was a victim of circumstance? Thought not.

Sixteen

Time - where does it go? When I was a child it seemed the summers were endless.

Seventeen

Christmas came. Clare, my fiancee, suggested we spend it with her parents. I told her my dad was ill and I needed to go to Wales - which was sort of true. I guess meeting Clare's parents was the next logical step on the road to an ongoing relationship. What the fuck is going on? Is this the way it's got to be? This adult life races on, somewhere along the line we take on commitments, make promises, pledges. Somewhere along the line our dreams and ambitions take a back seat to make way for the more sensible aspects of adult life; the reliable, responsible, grown-up world. Then one day you look behind and those dreams and aspirations are just memories. One day you look behind and a lifetime has passed you by...

Eighttteen

Back to poetry. The Beats, angst and ambiguity. We would meet, do our mad shows, but it seemed to be getting worse. Gene didn't have the same commitment, he was becoming unreliable. He seemed more elusive, more distant. Sure, when called upon he could still have the old gusto and go, but I was very unsure as to what was our next step.

People would ask us, "Hey, what's your bag?"

Gene loved replying, "A suitcase full of used fivers."

It sounded good to me. I think I was becoming a little confused. The whole trip was becoming a crazy exercise in chaotic confusion, I just had to trust someone, so I trusted G, I couldn't rely on my own judgement, and there certainly wasn't many of our peers that one could use as role models - poets just did not have attitude in those days. Yeah, sure Gene's ideas might be mixed up marketing scams, but they were the only plans anyone was offering to show me.

Look, you might be incredulous, yeah, go on shake your head in disbelief if you like. You probably think it's laughable how misguided I allowed myself to become. But truth is, nobody else was offering me much at all. Gene's ideas may have been a little cracked, but they included me. We were in the arena, fighting, together.

Let me ask you, who've you got shouting in your corner? Yes. No one has got a marketing scam for the product that is YOU. Yeah. It's no wonder that everyone gets the floor wiped with their dreams. Maybe we're all victims of circumstance. I mean, try writing a five year plan, right now. Yes, put this book down, go get a pad & pen, go on, and list those goals, anticipate the obstacles, work out your strategy. Five Years? Heavy!

Yeah, like you, most of the time I haven't got

a clue - I don't know where I'm really going - most of the time I don't even know where I am.

Right now I'm in Gelston point, a tower block in E1. In a flat on the 21st floor. It's February. I'm talking to Mike. I like Mike, I used to live with him in this very flat. Mike was an interesting guy; a London Underground tube driver in his mid twenties. He hardly drank any alcohol, was a karate black belt and a heavy dope smoker. Extremely articulate, an active communist, he could blind you with talk of Marxist theory and dialectical materialism which sounded gobbledegook to me. To top all this he looked like a young Steve McQueen, no I lie, he was better looking than Steve McQueen. Mike had a confident air, unlike the rest of us he seemed to know where he was going. I enjoyed the time I lived with Mike in this flat. After I'd moved out, Rhys had moved in.

Mike has just told me about Rhys attempting to jump out of the window. Fascinating as this story might be, I couldn't give a fuck. Rhys didn't jump, Mike managed to drag him back. This was all of two years ago. I came to see if Mike had any news on Gene. He'd seen him - scored some wicked bush. I did not want a smoke, thank you, but I'm angry (again) and I've got to track down the G. I like Mike, but I'm seriously pissed off, I make my excuses and leave. The lift is working!

I'm walking up Sidney Street, I was probably going to end up in Murphy's, and have a drink. Drink and try to forget. Where was Gene? I was becoming sick of this obsession. Who does he think he is? Then bang, coming round the corner, it's him.

"Where have you been?"

"What? Oh Spike, there you are. I've been looking for you. What a coincidence, a stroke of luck."

"Fuck the jive talk. What's the score?"

"Score? What score? One nil, two nil, who cares? What is this, an interrogation? I don't need this."

Gene feigns being seriously hurt and angry, he shrugs and begins to make a move away.

"Don't walk away, what makes you so special? What do you think gives you the right?"

Gene stops, he turns slightly towards me. He's rubbing his hand on his chin. I can see his mind is working overtime. Then in a deeply solemn voice he says, "Spike, look, stay cool, hang loose guy, everything is going to be OK... I'm planning our next step... the tour... Yes. Oh yes Spike... The Big City Beats Tour."

Amazing, here I am, on Shit Street E1, my head is spinning. I'm looking at Gene, impeccably dressed in a chocolate brown bomber with fur collar, black leather strides, dark glasses and gloves. A tour? My head overflows with questions, but before I can say anything. Gene turns and shouts, "Sorry Spike, got some business to attend to. Give my love to Veronica. You work on the structure of the set and bring your scribbles and thoughts to The Blind Beggar on Tuesday, see you there 8.30 sharp - must dash."

He was gone like the Lone Ranger. There was no silver bullet, only a silver lining left in my psyche by the exhilarating thoughts of Chairman Gene. Damn, I had so many things I wanted to say, so much I needed resolving. A tour? A tour of where? It didn't make any sense, and yet it made every sense. It sounded fantastic. The Beggar, Tuesday. A tour! My last girlfriend was called Janet, my fiancee's name is Clare. Who the fuck is Veronica? What about the video we were going to make?

Nineteen

Gareth and me are standing in Piccadilly Circus, at the corner of Regent Street and Piccadilly. Gareth's an old friend from South Wales. I'd met him in Cardiff in 1977, just after I'd moved down from Ponty. He'd been a drug dealer then. Punks liked speed, Gareth could get speed. Like the rest of us, he moved up to the smoke. He'd stopped dealing and was now working as a waiter in Wardour Street. Gar was some character, after a couple of drinks he got incredibly witty; razor sharp; told a good joke. Gar liked a drink. You just had to be careful when you were with Gar, that he didn't drink too much - he can become a bit of a liability.

The Dilly was a landmark, a reference point, a meeting place for the tourists that flocked to London. In summer they'd sit around in droves, on the steps encircling Eros, being slowly poisoned by exhaust fumes - a sad state of affairs. Even on these freezing cold winter days you could still guarantee a good gaggle of backpackers, so it was obviously an excellent place for buskers and a prime site for hangers-on, beggars and tea leaves. Boots by Burger King used to be a pick-up area for rent boys but it seemed to have been recently blitzed by the police.

Gar and I looked at Eros then up at the flashing neon signs advertising Fuji, Coke, Condoms.

We had come up West on Gareth's instigation. He said it would be just what we needed, a break from our East End worries and the bleak English winter that had gone on for far too long. Me? I was just waiting for Tuesday to roll around, when I could be with G and discuss our plans for stardom.

"Look at Bowie!" shouted Gar.

I searched the crowd but couldn't see any sign of the Thin White Duke.

"Where Gar, I can't see him?"

"There!" Gar pointed up into the sky to my left. "Doesn't he look pleased with himself?"

I looked upwards and on the corner of The Trocadero saw a waxwork model of Bowie, in his 'Young American' fuck-off shoulder pads, hands aloft welcoming the world to the capital.

"Hey Spike do you think they'll make waxwork dummies of us?"

Fucking mad question. Funny, but mad.

"Get real Gar, not unless you become a mass murderer or something. You know my Dad said to me if you can't become famous be infamous."

Gareth retorts - a wry smile on his face, "Crazy advice if you ask me, I'll be buggered, mass murderer? Alright then, the pub, is it? I could murder a pint... or two." Gareth can be quite funny a lot of the time.

Life moved briskly around us in the hustle and bustle of a chilly central London. There seemed to be an overload of humanity on the street.

"Alright Gar, lets get out of this hassle, somewhere quiet."

It must seem weird to you. Me and Gar going all the way up West for some action, and the first thing we do after emerging from the tube is to go into a boozer. I mean do we have pubs in

Whitechapel or what? I didn't even consider this question. Gar likes a pint.

A beggar shouted, "Spare some change."

We ignored him. We headed up Shaftesbury Avenue and took a left into Great Windmill Street with its flashing neon advertising strip and peep shows. We hit on the Red Lion pub next to a Malaysian restaurant. Inside the pub the clientele seemed to encompass the whole spectrum of Soho life. Gay boys, strippers and prostitutes on their break, heavy duty pimps and some that were really weedy and seedy. Pubs in Whitechapel were nowhere near as interesting as this. There was a strong Maltese faction that chatted about the cab business, though I never saw any taxis outside. The Maltese looked totally unapproachable, it was weird, they had this aura of streetwise machismo about them. Gar unsuccessfully attempted to talk to them about the taxi game, it was an avenue he thought he might like to pursue. He got nowhere. They gave him the advice to stay out of the cabbie business.

Gar had seen some sights but up in the West End he was the wide-eyed country boy, green as the grass from the Valleys of our birthplace, gawking like some tourist.

Suddenly he turns to me and with a loud voice declares, "Look at her, what a chest!"

"Shut up Gar, keep your bloody voice down."

"What?" He's staring at the well endowed brass at the next table, and he isn't paying the slightest heed to my words of caution. I try to act knowledgeable and cool, when really I'm awkward and embarrassed.

"Shush Gar. Look they're just in here for a quiet drink, it's not a freakshow. How would you like it if they came up East to gawk and stare at your flat?"

Gareth turned around with a big grin on his face, "They're welcome Spike, anytime, of course I would have to charge. Hey do you think any of the girls might be interested? We could do some kind of trade."

"What, see the finer features of Gareth's flat from the best vantage point; flat on their back." You can see the slates through the holes in Gareth's bedroom ceiling.

Gareth's obviously with me on this one; he laughs and chides, "Yeh, or come have a dump in the air conditioned ambience of the luxurious Throne Room." Gareth lived in a top floor flat in The Grove, with a smelly outside toilet on the balcony. It certainly wasn't the Hilton.

Gareth's chuckling away - he's feeling happy with the alcohol and bon homie. He's obviously enjoying the madness of our surroundings. His head swivels back towards the entrance, and he shouts, "Spike, look at that, it's a bloke."

I'd noticed the hairy transvestite who'd just strutted in, but when Gareth turns back towards me, I theatrically look over at a table of working girls, seated next to us.

"Which one?"

"Ooh hoh," chortles Gareth, "Funny man. Funny man. You'll be buying a round next."

We drank and drank too much. The lager flowed and the room spun, the crowd got more interesting, faces and images merged. Gar and I swayed to the jukebox sound which cranked out the old hits from the fifties onwards. We carried on the conversation of drinkers, conversation that covered all subjects and continents of the globe. We put the world to rights. Suddenly Gar said, "I feel horny."

"What?"

"Can't you feel it?"

"What the fuck are you on about?"

"This place, this area, it exists for sex. Soho Spike, Soho. Sex. I tell you Spike, I need some sex."

I look around, embarrassed, Gareth's voice is getting loud as the drink takes hold, but it's obvious nobody's really listening. I survey the clientele. "Well you've come to the right place, there's plenty on sale around here."

"Yes!" he exclaims.

He stands up so quickly he almost topples over.

"C'mon lets take a walk."

Gareth downed the remainder of his pint, and slammed down the empty glass. I couldn't quite put my finger on what was happening, but in hindsight I realise that Gar had somehow planned all this. It was all too theatrical, too excited, too rushed to be impromptu. I just got caught up in it all. We staggered out of the Red Lion and walked up to Brewer Street then took a right past the Raymond Revue bar. I didn't know where all this was going. Gar was pissed again, he kept saying, "C'mon, c'mon."

We were halted in our tracks when a young woman in a short leather skirt stopped us and asked the time. Gar tried to look at his watch. She looked pissed off, didn't even wait for his reply, but went into a rap, the like of which I have never heard before or since.

She said, "Look I can do two's, double is no problem. Of course it'll cost extra. I can take you one at a time or both together. You want mouth, arse, cunt I got it. I do hand jobs, blow jobs, if you want les it costs. I got a girlfriend back at the flat around the corner. Chains, whips, leather, animals, only dogs and only *my* dogs. Oral is twenty-five, a hand job twenty and full fuck fifty. Anal is a hundred. You want no condoms that's possible, but it'll cost. Together will be one hundred and fifty. If you want anything more kinky it'll cost. I can fuck you up the arse for sixty. You want les or a double routine with my girlfriend and it'll..."

"Cost?"

"OK comedian. Look I haven't got all night. You want something? You look like nice blokes."

I looked at Gar who was grinning stupidly. "Sorry lady we haven't got enough money."

"What?!" she declared. "You could 'ave fuckin' stopped me!"

Gareth held his palms upwards, made some cheesy grin and shrugged melodramatically. She looked at me. I probably looked as stupid as Gareth; I smirked, raised my eyebrows - looked heavenward.

"Arsehole Taffs," she growled and spat on the floor, then turned to walk away.

"Whooer!" shouted Gareth after her, then burst into an overstated laugh.

We watched in admiration as she walked away, her hand raised giving us the middle finger, without so much as a glance back. We stood there mesmerised, admiring her confident, arrogant, exaggerated wiggle disappearing into the crowd.

"Fuck me Spike, I'd sure like to have had me some of that."

"C'mon Gar let's go have another drink - one for the road."

"No Spike we're in Soho, we've got to go to a peepshow."

"You can go but count me out. Come on Gar, let's have a snifter."

"No. Oh c'mon Spike. Look I'll pay." Gareth pulled some crumpled notes out of his trouser pocket, held them in front of me. I furtively glanced from side to side, as I pushed his hand down. It felt unsafe to be waving cash around on these crazy streets.

"Alright." I agreed.

And the next thing I know we're in the alleyway at the end of Berwick Street. Gar's leading the way, weaving through the crowd, on a mission, like he's been here many times before. He stopped at a doorway which had a notice declaring '£1 a peep' scrawled on a fading yellow painted wall. He looked over his shoulder to see I was aware of his intention, then with an arm gesture beckoning me to hurry, he disappeared inside. I quickened my pace and without any time to consider what I was embarking on I entered through a multicoloured plastic strip curtain into a downbeat hallway.

Walking up the creaky wooden stairs, I hesitated for a moment, wondering what I was doing there - if it would make me or you feel any better I could blame it on the booze, on the haste and hustle which Gareth had used to entrap me - I could say I was easily led, and therefore not really responsible - I could say any fucking thing to ease our guilt, but truth is, like you, I was completely fascinated. Scared? Yes, but definitely, overwhelmingly fascinated.

I caught Gareth at the top of the stairs. A big black guy in a dog-tooth jacket had stopped him from going any further. "Yeah?" Gareth pulled out a ten pound note and gave it to this guy, who handed him some pound coins, eyed me suspiciously and said, "One cubicle each."

Gar remonstrated and explained we had to go and watch together. The black guy didn't look at all uneasy. Just said it would cost an extra tenner. I knew he was fleecing us, he knew he was fleecing us, but Gar paid up.

We walked along the woodchip and magnolia corridor, and into the booth. It stunk of cigarette smoke and semen, and contained an old tubular steel and vinyl chair. On the wall was a stainless steel box with a slot. A sign stated 'Pound coins only'. I closed the door.

Gar sat on the old chair and I stood behind him. The booth was smaller than your average toilet cubicle. Gar pushed a pound coin into the slot and a peephole opened. Gar craned his neck and pushed his face into the lighted slit. I watched like a voyeur, the drink in my system made it all seem otherworldly, the dark, the insanity of the situation... Gar said "fuck" and poured some more money in, he started to unzip his fly. I looked at the back of his neck. It was dark in the booth. The walls must be made out of cardboard - I am aware that there are also two people in the next cubicle.

There's tinned muzak from the room in front of the slot, there's a slight noise as Gareth's stroking his cock and breathing heavier - but I can distinctly hear a voice from the booth next to ours. I think it's the black guy who took our money, he's saying, "She's blond, small, but good shape, tanned. She's got a bra on, panties. She's pushing the panties to one side now - you can see the pubes, black. She's shoving her finger in her hole - in and out, in and out. Now she's licking her finger. Now she's put her hand back inside her panties. She's got one tit out now, she's squeezing it. Pushing and squeezing. Now she's licking her nipple and feeling her cunt. She's pushing down her panties, pulling her other titty out. She's bending down. She's picking up a vibrator now..."

Suddenly I am jettisoned back into what is happening in my own booth, by Gareth exclaiming, "It's Maria."

"What?" I say.

But Gareth's grunting and working away, panting. He's groaning her name, it's all very weird, hard to grasp. Then he's shouting "fuck, fuck" as he's trying to grab some more money which has spilled onto the floor. He's managed to get one more pound coin into the slot. I try to see through the peep hole but Gar's too hard into his crescendo to let me look. He moans again, "Oh *yes* **Maria!**"

I can tell he's come. Gar moves to one side, motioning me to the cavity, flickering with light.

I moved closer and looked into the hole, there was a woman wearing a blond wig who was masturbating herself with a vibrator. I looked hard at the side of her face. But she was turning away.

It could be Maria but it's difficult to tell.

Suddenly, a clunk and the aperture closes, the cubicle goes darker.

I watch in the half light as Gar wipes his dick with a hanky. We both look at each other like a couple of burglars caught in a police spotlight. We say nothing.

Gar zipped up and we left the booth and walked down the corridor towards the exit. Another black guy was stood at the head of the stairway. He looked us up and down with a menacing sneer and asked for a fiver. Gar started to argue, but this guy looked psychotic, his eyes widening as he reached inside his jacket. I got out my wallet. As I handed over the note I asked if I could speak to the girl. He looked me up and down and said for a hundred I could have ten minutes. I started to say something about only wanting to talk to her, but realised just how ridiculous I must have sounded. I said instead that I didn't have that kind of money. Then we heard a noise behind us, and we turned and watched as the other black guy held the cubicle door open as a white guy with sunglasses and a white stick tip-tapped down the corridor towards us.

"Goodbye gentlemen," said the bouncer as he slid the five into his jacket pocket.

"C'mon Spike." Gareth pulled my arm.

So we're on Wardour Street, heading south. I'm bubbling. Gareth seems a lot less pissed, his face determined and yet blank.

"Gar, are you sure - I mean positive it was Maria?"

"Of course I'm sure Spike. Look, don't say anything to Gene."

I wanted to talk more, but Gareth wasn't going to elaborate or speculate. It would have to pass, maybe it was Maria, maybe it was Gar's fantasy. We walked along Shaftesbury Avenue. I hailed a taxi, we entered and went back East.

Twenty

Eventually Tuesday came. Walking to The Beggar across the Cambridge Heath Road from Murphy's I was seized with a stupid surge of optimism. It was crazy. I was feeling crazy. I felt like something good was about to happen. I smiled and laughed out loud. No one looked at me, they probably thought I was another casualty to inner city insanity. They're probably right. Hope springs eternal. I entered The Beggar.

The Blind Beggar is a pub in Whitechapel Road; it has a certain notoriety. It was where Ronnie Kray had put two bullets in George Cornell's head, for calling him a 'fat poof'. Me and G had once been likened to Ronnie and Reggie in a review in City Limits.

Now I was waiting for Gene in The Blind Beggar. I wondered if it was an omen, a sign. Where was this discussion going to take us? Fuck knows. I had nothing on my horizon, except more of the same mundanity in my job in Whitehall. Apparently the Krays had a way with words, they could put on a passable performance, but when push came to shove they understood the sword was mightier than the pen, they understood how to flex a muscle. You couldn't rely on a pen saving you on the streets of E1, or in The Blind Beggar for that matter.

It was what we called a John's pub; strictly for white East End, tastefully decorated without being too gaudy. No dossers, winos or deviants in here. In the lunch hour it got the usual office types, by night the pub conversation had that secretive aura of a deal going down. Mine was with G. Dress was casual but smart. I got a drink at the bar and sat down waiting for Gene. The punters were sparse but huddled in groups. Nuggets of information were being passed on the ups and downs of E1.

"Look, I says to 'im, you can't punt that out down 'ere. Know what I mean? 'e says it's real good gear, schmutter, the business. Well, I says, I'll have your guts for garters if this is knocked off. E's insisting it's cabbage, no bleedin' labels. Anyways I said I'd see if it could be shifted. Got to be worth a monkey. Know what I mean."

"Maybe see you on that later Tone. See what we can do."

I tried to look disinterested with their conversation. Trouble with East End geezers, is a lot of them take this stereotyping too literally - they actually believe they *are* villains.

Where is G? He's getting to be late a bit too often lately. I looked at my watch and cursed him. I drank my beer, determined to shrug off my anger, but it was hard to convince myself to relax and enjoy my surroundings.

"Wot, ditched you has she?" A white Fred Perry type suggested.

"No, just waiting for a friend," I replied (wishing I could tell him to go fuck himself). Luckily the diamond geezer didn't want to pursue his line of enquiry. I stared at the burgundy flock wallpaper. Running through my head was the old Velvet's song, 'First thing you learn is that you always got to wait'; it keeps slipping into my head a lot just recently.

Then the door opens and in swans G, looking like a cross between a pimp and a fag. I've always admired his bravado in the wardrobe department; he's got some front. I try not to look over-enthusiastic to see him - I act cool - I'm burning inside.

"Gene. What'll you have?"

"Vodka Martini on the rocks."

God, he's pushing it at The Beggar - G's always pushing it. I'm the stupid that's got to order it from the bar. Fuck! The last time I'd had a drink with him he told me he wasn't drinking alcohol. Fuck! I swear, one day it's all gonna come back and slap him full in the face. But all that can wait till after the tour.

The Beggar crowd: "Get it sorted, cor blimey luv a duck, down the frog and toad to get a Ruby in me Derby".

I wondered if we registered. It's like nothing was said, but there was a feeling - I mean, some kind of feeling, that given half a chance - given any old excuse these people would happily vent their inherent hatred of anything different, and gaily bludgeon us to death. Diamond geezers. And us? Diamond geezers? Hardly. Gene's accent was some strange mish mash of hipster from around the globe - and I still had recognisable Valley Boy (*There's lovely, in eh?*). Diamond geezers? More like rough diamonds. Nothing a bit of cutting and polishing wouldn't put right, but one thing we liked to assume was we were sharp, we were ice. *Anyways Spike, it could possibly get hot - G's simmering - so just play it cool.* I was too paranoid for anything other than a swift one in the Blind Beggar...

"Vodka Martini on the rocks please," I say to the blond bosom behind the bar.

"Okey dokes luv," she says like it's perfectly normal, she even puts a green olive and a glacé cherry on a cocktail stick. I have a pint of lager - any lager. I take the drinks over to G and sit down.

"Well what's with this tour idea?"

"Spikes, chill out, it's just an idea right now - but it's a fucking good idea, don't ya think? We got to be ready Spike. Spike are you ready to be massive, cos that's what we're talking about here. We've got to be ready, after all, we can't run before we learn to walk."

Gene's getting me going. There's the inspired madness I always rise to, the tempting prospect that anything is indeed possible if you want to believe it can happen. "Spike, are you ready?"

"Yeah, I'm ready." *What the fuck am I saying?*

"Yeah Spike, yeah. It's gonna be mega - mega, my man. The minutiae needs to be worked on, but we're talking some serious shit here; TV, Film, Plays, T-shirts, Groupies... Spike are you tough enough?"

Gene is leaning forward, talking in low conspiratorial tones. He must have been a salesman somewhere along the line - not that I was a difficult proposition - I'm drawn in, I raise my eyebrows a little, but I'm drawn in. G knows me.

"Give people what they want. Better still, make 'em believe, Spike. Make 'em believe that what we got is really what they want."

I'm trying to look nonplussed, but... G knows me.

"The first thing we need to do is really hone down our act, get it razor sharp. Spike we got to be the very best we can possibly be. Are you ready?

"Yeah, yeah, get on with it," I say. I'm doing my best to not look too easy.

"Spike, I've got to be able to rely totally on your commitment here."

"OK. OK," I say, "we get razor sharp."

"Yes, razor sharp, hardened steel. Then we market the product; get professional, ruthless. We do not compromise. We sell ourselves, but Spike... we do not sell ourselves short."

Gene's eyes have not moved from mine all this time. His face is determined, his voice level and earnest. He was boring into me, forcing me. I look down at the table top.

"Get positive Spike. Get PMT."

"Pardon?"

"Positive Mental Attitude. Positive Mental Attitude. For fuck's sake guy, what else is going on for you these days? Haven't I always told you? You know what to do."

"Look in the mirror, and shout, 'Damn I'm good'?" I was attempting to be facetious here, but the G didn't notice - ***he was going...***

"That's the spirit. That's the old Spike I love. Look, we can't get cynical, I tell you, everyone's going to be buying, everyone. People are desperate Spike, desperate, they're all scrabbling about being Yuppies cos they've got nothing 'cept money to believe in. We've just got to make ourselves available, show 'em that we are, indeed, all that they want; everything they could possibly want. Everybody dreams Spike, everybody dreams of having something or someone to believe in. Belief Spike; you can't beat it. Spike!"

"Look Gene it all sounds very nice but nobody knows who the fuck we are. Nobody really cares." I'm positive that G has indeed noticed the incredulity I've been feigning, but he's not letting on.

"Yes Spike, yes! Exactly. Surprise Spike; you

can't beat it. Sure we're an unknown quantity, but Spikey, can't you see, that's a plus; a big mother of a plus. Surprise is the very key to success... Surprise is our watchword; we've got to keep them excited, keep them gagging, keep them wondering what are these boys gonna do next?"

"Good question." More irony from me, ***but the G's going...***

"Look, the way I see it is... we can't lose. Spike, the way I see it is the way everyone should see it. Most important of all Spike, the way I see it is the way you've *got* to see it. Sure Spike, I know everyone thinks I'm a crazy dreamer, or a loser, but Spike, this thing can't lose... We're winners Spike, winners. Life's a gravy train for some, and crap for others, lots of others. No crappola city for us Spike. Are you listening?"

"Yeah, I'm all ears." ***Gone!***

"Good. Spike, it's like the crap they feed us on TV. Look at America Spike. Look at the way they fill air time. I mean it's all bloody game shows. Game shows. While Joe and Jane Public moan about the rubbish that's offered - and this is the important bit Spikey - they still fucking well tune in. They just sit there and watch crap. While the TV station owners laugh all the way to the bank, and Mr and Mrs Gameshow Host are raking it in, riding in first class style on the Pullman Gravy Train. It's a bigger con than The Great Train Robbery - in fact it's daylight robbery... Here, isn't this the place where Ronnie Kray did the business?"

A couple of local lads look inquisitively in our direction, but nothing is said. G is oblivious; he's into overdrive with his description of his vision of our future success.

"Well, I'm behind the tour idea, but Gene, I mean as long as we keep ourselves grounded here... I mean as long as we don't get taken in ourselves."

"That's cool. Everyone gets hotter than a vindaloo, and we'll be... We'll be like ice. Ice Spike. Straight from the fridge freezer. Cool. Just like the cubes in this here martini. Hey this calls for a celebration, let me buy you a drink partner."

"Yeah, OK, same again, a lager."

God, I'd heard these spiels so often from the G, but it didn't matter. It was infectious, his optimism always cascaded over me and carried me along in the slip stream. Usually it was whooshing up like a rocket, a massive blaze of pyrotechnics and then down like a charred stick. This time, for some reason it felt different. It wasn't his manic glare or enthusiasm, I couldn't put my finger on it, but there was too much conviction... Yeah Gene could be showy, almost theatrical, but this time he had a serious intent in his wordplay; through all the airy fairy hyperbole there was a real gravity… this *was* SERIOUS.

Look, I'm not blameless in the making of these madcap endeavours, where we'd tilt at windmills like Don Quixote & Sancho Panza. Gene surges - I encourage, Gene oozes - I keep pumping, Gene charges - I'm behind him, slapping him on the back. One day this horse will be run into the ground and I guess we'll both be to blame for egging each other on. Who had the stick? Who had the carrot? Right now it didn't matter; I was feeling good. I'm sat in the Blind Beggar enshrouded in a magically warm glow of optimism, believing that if you dreamed something hard enough, often enough, then dreams might come true.

I watch Gene swagger to the bar. While he's waiting to be served he's engaging the local boys in some banter. They're laughing away. Gene buys them a drink. He's bought a drink for the barmaid. He's laughing and lollygagging like some regular.

I hear him say, "At least you could walk safely in the streets when the Krays were kings."

Everybody round the bar is nodding sagely. Gene turns away beaming. He rolls toward me, exuding confidence and charisma. It's time for me to oil the G machine.

"Go on Gene. Tell me more."

"Yeah, Spike, yeah. Look we've buggered about in the London scene for far too long - been there, done that, bought the T-shirt. Now it's time to hit the UK. Main targets will of course be the major cities; Newcastle, Leeds, Liverpool, Manchester, Edinburgh, Belfast. Then the English-speaking world. Hey Spike have you ever been to New York?" (G knew I hadn't).

"Yey, how'd you like to stay at the Chelsea Hotel? You'd love it. Spike, they don't know it yet but the world needs us. There are times in history when things need to be said and done. Times when it feels that there's a synchronicity, a moment, a special moment. That time is right now. It's time to act. Stop and hesitate, or pause to weigh up all your options and ZAP - the moment is over; passed and gone. Sure, you can wait for the next time, but... and this is the crucial thing Spike... there may never be a next time. This is our moment Spike. I see it. I feel it in my bones. This *is our time*. We have to grasp this very special moment with both our hands Spike. We have to hold on hard, and run with it."

G folds his arms and smiles to himself, looking like the cat who's got all the cream. He seems at one with the world, knowing he's about to change it. For a moment the Blind Beggar and its clientele dissolve into the haze of reality, leaving just me and the G in a magical world of possibilities.

Gene smiles the most alluring smile and raises his cocktail glass towards my pint. "To the tour."

We chink our glasses, then swig our drinks in one. Suddenly Gene rises, "Sorry Spike, must go point Percy at the porcelain. Back in a jiff." N.B. wrong time frame – G gets from toilet to bar too quickly!!

I'm left. I look around, and I'm back in the Blind Beggar, it's as if cold water has been poured all over me. I think about my job, my fiancée. I begin to think about the reality of my responsibilities, and then I begin to doubt the validity of the whole tour idea. Neither G nor me know anything about organising a tour. We've got no connections, nobody does poetry tours. I notice the Fred Perry is sat at the next table on his own, he's staring at me. He winks. I hear a shout from the bar, "Same again Spike?"

I glower back at the lonely weirdo, then turn to watch G's approach, but he's having a laugh with the barmaid. I hear him declare unashamedly that he's seen her in EastEnders on television, and he thinks she's gorgeous. She's lapping it up. He gives her his money and when she hands his change he clasps her hand for a long moment, and declares loudly, that she must keep the change, and buy a G & T, cos she's got to be the most radiant TV star he's ever seen. She's shaking her head but going all googly eyed and even blushing. Gene turns with a massive grin across his face. He sees he's attracted some attention from the regulars. He catches Fred Perry's eye. "She's gorgeous," declares Gene, "Absolutely gorgeous".

I got to give it to G, he does what he wants to do, on his own terms, he goes out on a limb, quite naturally, he takes a risk, and truth is he's still standing. Somehow he's managed to free himself from this muffled Britishness that traps us all, but at what cost? Maybe that's what living should be about, doing what you really want to do. The path of least resistance is comfortable, but maybe an easy life is living death. Is there life after life? Nobody knows - nobody. Most people in this culture should ask themselves, 'Is there life during life?'

I stuck with the G cos too much of my life was the path of least resistance - comfortable and safe. Gene chose a life on the edge; he'd gotten this far. He believed that we could make a tour work. Sure there were impediments and handicaps, but as Gene was fond of saying in his newly acquired assault speak, "It's better to die on your feet than to live on your knees". I had doubts - I had plenty of doubts. 'Everything is negotiable' was one of Gene's new stock phrases. Everyone was selling a line in those days - I could only give it a try - I wasn't signing a contract, this was not a deal that I would be unable to renege on. *Fuck it*, I thought to myself.

"Hey, Gene, it's my birthday. Today I'm thirty."

"Aw really? Spike, you should've told me. What a day to remember Spike - what a day. A fantastic new decade. I'm gonna get you something stronger than lager. Spike, come on my man, get that down your neck. The Big City Beats go multinational *and* it's your birthday."

He went back to the bar, loudly declaring to the whole pub that today was my birthday. He bought me a double brandy and swaggered back knowing he has all the eyes of The Beggar at his back.

"Come on Spike, you're only young once," Gene booms.

"Fuck it," I laugh, and the G laughs too. He stands up, raises his martini glass to the ceiling. I also stand, caught up in the headiness of it all.

"Fuck it," Gene declares.

"Fuck it," we declare in unison.

"Fuck it." I turn to see Fred Perry raise his pint pot.

"Fuck it," I hear from the bar and turn my head to see the barmaid's G & T held high.

"Fuck it!" And everyone in the bar joins in.

Fuck it!

So the drink flowed, and I began to discard the negative as Gene highlighted the positive. G's picture of world domination was so vivid and bright. If he had any doubts, he certainly wasn't going to share them with me; not yet anyway.

Suddenly he stops what he's doing and says, "Spike, what date is it?"

"It's February the 14th - it's me birthday," I gush stupidly.

"Valentine's Day - fuck it's Valentine's day. Maria. Fuck."

I slur, drunkenly, "If she loves you, she can wait. It's onwards Gene, for the Beats, it's onwards." I knew this would side-track him. It was the beginning of one of his lyrics.

"Yes Spike, yesss," he rapturously declares, "Onwards, upwards, towards tomorrow, towards the sky...”

Oh no. I close my eyes and think G is going to give a complete rendition of the BCB to the Beggar crowd. I’d seen him do worse in the past and get away with it. Luckily for us, even in our present state, G is aware of the cultural obstacles of overcoming the Beggar boys with performance poetry. I open my eyes to watch G rise and walk over to the gang of guys at the bar. “Ronnie and Reggie; God bless ‘em, real goodfellas, diamonds, the best. They loved their dear old mum.”

They look at him as if he’s a little demented and a lot pissed - they’re right. An old fella cackles in the corner, stands to attention, then raises his glass.

“God bless ‘em.”

G does a wobbly pirouette and flounces for the exit, me straggling behind holding his coat, trying to give an impression of not being unnerved.

I’m surprised when we’re out on the street to see the G do a hard right; his home and Maria were left.

So we’re high on Whitechapel Road; The Strip. Gene, like a protective brother, envelops me with one arm around my shoulder, and with an emphatic sweep of his free arm declares, “One day Spike, all this will be yours.”

I look around at the debris and decay of the market, downtown E1 and wonder if I want it.

“Don’t look so puzzled matey, this is the raw ingredients that make us what we are. This is life Spike, raw life. A tagliatelle of lies and torment. It’s our bread and butter Spike. Reality baguette. Take a bite my man. Don’t it taste good.”

I laugh out loud at G’s culinary analogies.

"Nah, tastes like a shit sandwich to me."

"Spike, oh Spike. Where's your imagination. You cynical old fool. Just cos you're thirty don't mean you gotta get all bitter and twisted. Romance Spike - it's Valentine's Day - where's the romance? Look. See that old wino over there? For all we know he's lived the most exciting, extravagant lifestyle. Yeah, sure he's down now, sure he's beat, hanging on the ropes at the edge of the ring. Sure nobody loves a loser Spike. That man there, he might be down, and out for the count, and the world walks on by Spike... But who knows Spike, who knows? Next week we may see him cruising in his limo, eating caviar and oysters, drinking champagne from a glass slipper."

"Have you been taking drugs?"

"Er, oh waddya mean? No Spike no. I'm on the best drug of all Spikey, it's the drug of life. Hey you should try some. Live it to the full, be generous, be adventurous, be brave... be a Big City Beat .. yee hee hee!"

With his upbeat assessment and free advice, G walks straight up to the dosser and produces a £5 note. He's waving it at the old tramp, whose taken completely aback, and so am I.

"Ere mate. What you think you're doing?" Gene's grabbed his grimy hand and is forcing the fiver into it. Gene stands back and smiles benignly. "Ey, what is this? This ain't dodgy is it; counterfeit rubbish?"

He's smoothed it out and is holding it up to the street lamp's rays. He's feeling its texture and examining it as if he worked in Lloyd's bank.

"If this is a snide, you can shove it. You hear me mister, you can wipe your arse with it."

The most bizarre mime show ensues, as the two remonstrate. Gene masquerades bemusement, and the old boy indignation as the five pound note is pushed and proffered back and forth. The G is giggling and shoe shuffling, pulling faces. Finally the wino crumples the note, puts it into his tattered coat and shouts, "Fuck off you queer."

"God, he could have been a bit grateful," I say to G as he links my arm and waltzes away.

"Every day there's a new lesson to be learnt Spike. You gotta take the rough with the smooth. Don't fret. Poor old fucker had every right to be upset, it was a dodgy bluey anyway."

We laugh out loud, we walk together up the strip. The G's just digging everything, he keeps breaking into a crazy little dance. I'm wanting more details of the proposed tour, but Gene's not in a mood to tell. He's moved on, he's moved elsewhere. My questions are either evaded or plain ignored. Gene wants a good time. He keeps laughing and singing. He keeps hugging me, giggling. Gene's out there with the angels, dancing on the pinpoint of a needle.

Suddenly Gene stops dead.

"Let's go to Murphy's," he declares, and we do a drunken about-face and march down the strip towards The White Hart, or Murphy's as us locals called it - *'Locals' What the fuck am I saying? I must be drunk.*

I'd started my evening in Murphy's, it had been quiet, I'd had a pint and a laugh with Gareth. Neither of us mentioned our outing up West. Gareth likes to have a laugh - not to get too serious. You got to catch Gar on the early shift though, when he starts into his fourth pint it's time to find your fun elsewhere - unless you wanna be with an obnoxious, bitter and twisted, maudlin drunk.

So we fall through the door to the Lounge - *huh, there's an misnomer, if there ever was one.* Somehow Murphy's had slipped through the net when the re-styling of East End boozers was booming. The Lounge at Murphy's would not even rate as 'shoddy bar' in the 1980's Britain 'Good Pub Guide' criteria. No doubt, in its day it had been quite an elegant drinking establishment, but that day was probably post war - and I'm talking about the first world war here - with its high ceilings, brass candelabra chandeliers, etched windows, mahogany and mirror panelling. It was now a mis-matching of dark wood tables and chairs, balancing precariously on worn, dirty, flesh-coloured linoleum. Black fag burns in everything. Broken, etched and cut windows, now replaced with bobbled toilet window glass. Broken bevelled mirrors replaced with plywood, or not replaced at all - but it suited a certain clientele; some old Irish, and then some younger, hard drinking, East End immigrants - the Grovers. It suited the likes of Gareth. Gareth had been banned from everywhere, for being a complete obnoxious drunken arsehole. He'd never been banned from Murphy's.

Gareth was the first thing we set eyes on. He woke up from a nod just as we entered, and grunted, "Hey, the fucking White Brothers. Yea, hoh, yea. Fuckers."

Luckily we managed to see Andy and Rhiannon, two of the old Grove faces, across the room, and we made a bee line over. I heard Gareth grumbling insults, I didn't turn round.

The Murphy's crowd is in high spirits. It's

already closing time, but nobody looks like they're going anywhere. G's happy, he's smiling and waving hello's to the folks he knows. Then he's talking to Barry - I don't like Barry, he's a Bethnal Green boy born and bred, a crook, a dodgy geezer; Gene and him have their faces close, no smiles - it's definitely not a "Hi, how are you" conversation. I'm close to the bar.

"Gene. Drink?"

"Yeah Spike, thanks."

I'm at the bar and there's Susie. G used to live with Susie. I kind of stay in touch with her. She's well drunk. Susie's weird - *Fuck, everyone's weird, but tonight it's my birthday, and the night air in Murphy's is awash with alcohol and to-hell-with-it forgetfulness.* Susie's normally incredibly quiet, and nervous, but after a few drinks she becomes all fluttery-eyed flirty - it's a bit sad really - but I like it. She's coming on all naïvey, ooh, I'm all bubbly and helpless and sexy. Tonight it's all just fine by me. I'm coming on all boyish, man-about-town, wouldn't mind a shag down some dark alley, drunk.

At some point I look up and notice everything's the same but things have changed around. Some people are exactly where they were, but they're engaged in conversations with different people, or the same people, and others are not where they were, but they're elsewhere laughing and stuff, with other people orbiting around. It all seems more lock-in, more intimate than it did. We're all on our missions to oblivion - special camaraderie.

I see that Gene has been cornered by Gar, and G's kinda trapped, and Gar's smoking, and swaying, and a pint in one hand and he's pointing and prodding G, and G is trying to look like it all don't mean anything, and he looks trapped.

And there's Susie, and she's just laid her head on my shoulder, and she's sighing, and fluttering, and bowing her head all girlie, girlie, and I remember I must buy G & me a drink, so I turn around, but the barman is serving and lollygagging in the bar area. Susie puts her hand on my chest, I put my arm round her waist. I catch the barman's eye, he ambles over, smiling at some joke some Irish dosser on the end-of-the-bar barstool has told him.

"Ah yus, me fine fella, and what can I be doin' for yous?"

"Two pints of lager please."

"To be sure."

"Susie?"

Susie, has turned her attention to some tall blond, longhaired guy whose come up to the bar. She doesn't hear me, she's fluttering her eyes and being all seductive and naïve and girlie, girlie. I get the drinks and turn towards G's corner. The wave of chattering and laughing and clinking and smoke and nicotine yellow and dull light and drunkness lifts me upward. It's my birthday. I'm in Murphy's. Everybody's having a lock-in time, and I just want to laugh or shout out loud. I just love everybody. I just find the exhilaration, the thrill... I just find everything... I just find it all so amusing.

I get up to G and there's a different feeling, a panic in me. I can tell Gene is seriously pissed off. Gareth is being accusative, and argumentative; he's lapsed into his usual drunken tirade, prodding G and emphatically declaring (accusing?) how The White Brothers could have gotten somewhere if only they'd listened to him. Gareth is fucked, he's all crimpled and blinking and belligerent. Whenever Gareth gets this drunk, and G is in the vicinity, he always seeks out the G, like some lobotomised assassin, batters Gene with his vitriolic resentments and insecurities. I dunno why he feels so bitter and jealous, not really, but he does, and whenever he gets this pissed, he insists on berating the G unmerciously. I think Gareth hates himself - I don't blame him!

I hear Gareth saying, "...and all this nigger rap shit, and Steve Strange poncy bollock backing tracks. I told you Gene.."

I interject, trying to sound all breezy, up tempo, "La-dee-da. Lah-deeh-dah." It works, briefly.

Gareth sees me, he's wobbling his head, in what he probably thinks is some haughty, superior, caddish way. "Spike. Spikey. Fucking..."

Gene clasps his hand around the proffered pint, then moves quickly, sideways, slides out of Gar's tunnelled peripheral vision, walks over towards Susie and the blond-haired guy.

"The White Brothers. The White Brothers-s-s. Yah!" Gareth's trying to be all cynical au fait, sneering, imitating a chant we used on stage.

"Yah!" I retort, and cackle like it's all just a joke, doesn't mean anything.

Gareth staggers and sways around like some punch drunk never-was, then falters as he tries to locate the disappeared G man. Fuck knows how he managed to stand for so long. He topples. His cigarette hand swishes backward, catching Nigel in the cheek, then forward, dislodging my lager all over me, Andy, Rhiannon... His legs buckle, his elbows go out, he half falls but jams himself between two tables. He's managed to cause a massive amount of grief, while preserving his half full beer glass from spilling. He whoops. Nobody else thinks it's funny - not at all. I reach down and grab him under the armpits, I kind of half lift, half push him onto the maroon ripped leatherette seat that runs along the back wall - people slide away either side. Gareth whoops again, and does this very Garethish-(when pissed)-type Bruce Lee cat-like "Ee-oow!"

I've seen this before, Gareth's gone. He isn't really aware of anything. He's always aware of his drink. He looks through slitty, puffed eyes, and mutters something, swigs the remaining beer, burps, begins a cracked rendition of 'Maria', laughs, puts his head down on his chest and (thank fuck!) sleeps; back on the nod; where he was when we walked in, sad and lonely. A sad and lonely drunk.

And I am drunk too. I look around, and suddenly things begin to blur; voices blend to a babble, the cacophony is tumbled and echoing, and the yellow light and brown and flesh and maroon and it's all whirling, and I'm gonna pass out or something. My remaining semblance of sense tells me to *get to the fucking bog*, I figure if I can just get in to the cubicle and close the door, then I can black out or vomit or fall to my knees or die, something degrading and serious and something I needed to do in private.

I make my way to the door that leads to the corridor where the steps descend to the basement - the men's toilets. It's all impounding. The darkness of the corridor after the yellowed flurry, is like a death tunnel, like a black voodoo drum, like the ominous heartbeat of doom. I think I'm gonna have to just slump down. Everything is breathing in on me, I'm bending lower as I move forward, my shoulder against the wall. I make it to the top of the stairs, they're steep. I try to make a grab for the banister rail. Too late. I end up at the bottom, on the stone flags. I feel the warm saltiness of blood in my mouth. I stand up, all giddy. I feel hurt, but I don't feel nauseous any more.

So I'm stood pissing, there's no mirror in these toilets, blood is dripping into the urinal. I'm drunk. I'm transfixed watching blood droplets mingling with the piss stream, and streaking into the yellowy-brown urinal bottom, on its way down to the fag-butt cluttered hole. I'm drunk. I don't think I'm thinking anything. Then suddenly, or not - I'm drunk - Gene is behind me.

"Spike, I've fucked."

I turn, I'm bleeding, my lip's bleeding, and the basement bog at Murphy's is disgusting, and Gene says, "You're bleeding!" and pulls a hanky out of his breast pocket. And I'm saying there's no bog roll, and Gene takes his hanky and puts a finger into his mouth and wets one corner, and he's wiping blood off my cheek, my chin.

"Spike it's Valentine's Day."

"Yeah," I say, "my birthday."

"Spike, can I sleep at yours?"

"Fuck, yeah..."

"It's just Maria's gonna kill me..."

"Fuck yeah," I say, I mean I'm drunk. Everything seems OK to me.

G grabs my head in both his hands, pulls my face towards him and kisses me, full on the lips. I'm cut. I'm drunk. I like it. I don't care. There's something sexy about having a broken lip kissed better. It's weird. Gene laughs out loud. We both laugh.

We ascend the stairs, and back into the Lounge; it seems brighter, louder, spirits are high. Some time in it all the whole room erupts into a spontaneous rendition of 'Happy Birthday' to me. I have a sensation of floating.

I'm drunk. Gene's drunk. Murphy's is having a lock in. It's my birthday. Everyone is buying me drinks, I think, I'm buying everyone drinks, I'm dancing on the bar to a Madonna record:

"Like a virgin// Touched for the very first time..."

I've got a tea towel wrapped around my head. I've got a floppy bunny shoved down the front of my trousers. I'm drunk. I kind've just got up on the bar, cos I wanted to get away from Gar, whose woken up again, and he's getting more and more abusive towards Gene, but also more and more incoherent and useless. Gene's tryna have a good time; trying to forget. Gareth's just remembering, and it's just horrible and pathetic to witness. Gareth's a drunk, and he's going nowhere, and Gene's my friend, and maybe he's going nowhere, but it's my birthday, and I don't want this. I want respite. Gareth's slurred, whingey, vitriol is wearing everything/everyone down. I'm scared he's going to say something - I don't want that. And so I hear the opening bars of the old Madonna song; that jaunty bass riff...

"I've made it through the wilderness// Somehow I made it thru-oo-hoo..."

and I don't know; it means something - I'm not sure what. I'm all maudlin and happy and sad, drunk, and I just wanna forget; take the heat off

Gene and the trouble and the worry of this shit life, and I'm not sure of where I'm going, or where I've come from, and then I'm up on the bar counter, and everyone is clapping and jeering, and I'm up there, high in the smoke and lights and cheering, and I look down and there's Gareth, drunk and bleary and fucked, but he sees me, and stops haranguing Gene, and he's shouting something that he thinks is probably funny, his blotched head moving like some badly animated reptile - he does that when he's drunk, but it doesn't matter what shite Gareth's shouting, cos nobody's listening, nobody's looking, they're all watching me - and I'm up there; high. And somebody turns up the music...

"I was beat// Incomplete// I'd been had// I was sad and blue// But you made me fee-e-e-l// Yah, you made me feel// Shiny and new-hu..."

And I've got a beery, wet tea towel wrapped round my head, and I've got this worn out, tiny floppy bunny shoved down my waistband, and I hear some girls in the corner woo-hooing, and I know I should be gyrating sexy or something, but instead I'm on the bar counter, and I pull up my trousers and hitch the bottoms up, over my knees, and I'm there with my hairy shins and socks and shoes, and I'm doing some kind of knees-up/David Byrne 'Road To Nowhere' type thing, and everyone is clapping, and singing the chorus...

"Like a virgin// Touched for the very first time// Like a vir-hir-gin..."

And the Woo-hooing girls are all smiling and together with their arms wrapped around each other and they think they're the Chiffons or Supremes or some pastiche of some girlie backing singers, and everyone's digging it, and even

Gareth's stood up, one hand on hip, the other pointing a finger at the ceiling, like he thinks he's imitating John Travolta in 'Saturday Night Fever', and he's shouting his Bruce Lee-type me-ow whoop thing all the time, out of time. It's me and Madonna and Murphy's, and I kind of get carried away and start whirling round, and I'm gone, and I don't know what I'm going to do when the song ends, but it doesn't matter the whirling takes care of that, and as another chorus climaxes I just fall backwards, somehow expecting everyone will catch me. I'm a star.

CRASH.

I hit a table full of glasses.

Twenty·one

I wake up in a taxi. Gene's next to me. He smiles. I've got 'Like A Virgin' still in my head. Gene puts a reassuring hand on my shoulder, "It's OK Spike. You're OK."

So we're being driven down the Mile End Road, on our way to my place. I live in an estate on the periphery; Blackwall Tunnel Northern Approach - it's where our East End finishes and an easier, quieter East End progresses to Essex and into the sea...

Twenty-two

Some things have happened in my life. Some things that happened and I don't know if... Oh I'm sure you, dear reader, have had things happen to you - things you'd rather not have happened - you know, those events that haunt you - when you did the wrong thing, said the wrong thing, were in the wrong place at the wrong time, and... things happened to you - and all life is experience, and we as human beings, whoever we are, are the result of those experiences - good - bad - indifferent.

Shame. A word that is used in different ways. Shame. A word that is often used inappropriately. "It's a shame." Do you know the difference between shame and guilt? Buggered if I do. So you were afraid, you were angry, you were drunk, stoned, naïve, you were hasty, reckless, greedy, stupid... and you did something you would never have done if you could have considered better, weighed up the options, had time or opportunity to get a better perspective... But you did it - you did it, and that is that. And now you are ashamed, you feel guilty now. And unfortunately our lives are not on video tapes that we can watch when we want to, or erase and record something else. They rewind in our memories, and we have no control.

Sometimes in the quiet time, without warning certain memories return. And you shudder. You shout out loud, try to stop them. Anything's better than those memories just rising, darkly, pervading your whole mind - shout out loud into the quiet dark, to try and return to the real world of sounds and senses - not memories and feelings - memories and feelings of guilt, of shame.

How can we rid ourselves of guilt and shame? Fuck knows! Maybe if you're Catholic you can say ten hail Mary's on your knees. Does it work? Maybe. What would I know? Maybe you can spend years in intensive therapy, going backwards - getting angry, admitting, grieving, crying - but when all the rituals and emotion, all the shouting and crying and talking and intellectualising; when all that is ended, you still just have to live with it.

Some people can't live with it, and they kill themselves.

This is not a confessional. Like you... I live with it.

Twenty-three

The taxi pulls up and we clamber out. My head aches. I'm knackered.

We're in my flat. I've told Gene he can sleep in my bed. He's suddenly picked up - fuck knows how - I thought he'd drunk as much as me. It's 1.30am, I've got work tomorrow and Gene's wide awake.

"Spike, I'm gonna smoke some smack to unwind. Want some?"

The last time I smoked heroin I was sick as a dog. I liked it, but I was sick as a dog. I'm knackered. G's wide awake and offering me free heroin. It's my birthday, I've got work in the morning. Fuck it!

"OK, but not too much, I don't wanna be sick."

We sit on the bed - G's got everything with him - foil, all neat and folded in his wallet - smack, in a small wrap he's removed from somewhere in the lining of his jacket.

"Hey Spike, it's your birthday, I got some free base."

"OK," I says. I don't know what 'base' is, but it's free - what the fuck. Most of my drug use has been done on the basis of being given something for free by friends - it's not going to kill me. G knows I can't abide hallucinogens, so I figure whatever it is he's planning to give me has got to be reasonably OK.

"OK," I says, and look knowingly excited at the two small packets G has produced.

G smooths out the foil on a brand new paperback copy of 'Money' by Martin Amis, which I had just started reading. G, of course, notices, and makes a comment of approval - that makes me feel good. He'd read the hardback version. He didn't seem to remember it was his recommendation that persuaded me to buy it.

G tears the foil, so he's got one piece about 7" x 3", and another smaller strip (about 5" x 3"). The small sheet he rolls around a pen barrel, to make a thin tube, then he gets out a lighter and heats the underside of the larger piece of foil. Then he taps out brown powder from one wrap, and white crystals from the other. He offers me a smoke, but I say he should go first - I want to see how to do it properly - last time I smoked off the foil I couldn't quite get the flame movement, and sucking through the mouth, and breathing through the nose, and everything, quite right.

So G applies the flame under the foil, and the brown & white melt into each other, and then G tilts the foil slightly as the flame plays under the molten blob, which leaves a black trail as it runs down the foil, and G follows the blob with his foil tube, sucking in the smoke, a knowing, satisfied suck, then he stops, with a lung full, and he holds it down, for as long as he's able. He looks like a wooden Indian - stiff - smug - noble.

Now he's beckoning me over - flapping - all irritated. He's got the foil tube in his mouth, he's pointing at it, at me, he's like a man underwater with no breath left. I move closer, and he grabs me round the neck and he pulls me close. I open my lips and G guides in the silver tube. He blows. I suck. It's weird; there's the taste of piss and alcohol, and it's warm and damp and stale. I cough and retch immediately.

"Aw Spike. You're supposed to hold it in!"

Fuck, I'll never be into drugs. You've really got to have a particular mind set to smoke or sniff or snort smelly and vile concoctions just to get high. I've always been a non-smoker, I've always wondered how those boys behind the bike sheds at school persevered. I just didn't have it in me.

So eventually Gene gives me a little pile of powder and crystal, and he hands me the tube and his lighter, and I do my best, and it's not brilliant - I splutter, and burn the wrong blob at the wrong time - but whatever, some gets into my lungs - and I begin to feel good.

Gene smokes some more, and I accept and hold in his blowbacks.

Then I'm smoking, much more confidently, and I'm thinking I should offer G a blowback. He sucks on my second-hand smoke and goes, "Ooh."

The next thing I know is the tube is forgot and it's like we're kissing, 'cept I'm blowing and he's kind of sucking - and I'm getting excited, and so's G.

Fuck me!!

So we're kissing, and then G's pulling me tight, and his hand's on my thigh and he's rubbing me, and I'm squirming and kissing and enjoying it - lost. And G moves his hand onto the bulge in my pants, and he's kneading, gently, firmly - in the moment, the moment.

Gene slides his hand down inside my waistband. I undo my flies. I push up G's roll neck sweater; it's soft, good quality. He's got a hairy chest; I rub it; rub my fingers through. He's holding my throbbing cock, kind of gently massaging the moist tip with his thumb. I feel so warm and safe and sexy. G seems to know what he's doing, and it's like nothing is required of me. And I'm undoing the buckle and the button and zip, and his trousers fall to his knees. I'm sat on the bed, he's stood before me. I push down his trunks, clasp his buttocks, pull him toward me. His cock is in my mouth. I'm gripping his arse cheeks. He's kind of still, but sighing, panting, softly. My head moving back and forth - sliding - my mouth an 'o'. G's got his hands on my shoulders - gripping. I close my eyes. I like it.

Gene's breaths are getting shorter. Then he gasps softly, "No Spike, no."

I get all self conscious, stop moving.

Gene sees my confusion and croons. "No Spike, I'm gonna come. What about you Spike? What about *you*?"

I dunno. I hadn't thought about me.

G's stood there. I'm sat there. Gene removes his shoes and his trousers from off his ankles. He kneels on the floor before me. He removes my shoes. He undoes my buttons, then tugs off my jeans. I lie back on the bed, lift up my bum; help him; push my trousers and Y-fronts down my legs.

Ooh - ooh!

G's kissing my ankles, my knees - licking his tongue down the inside of my thigh. I just lay there, squirming slightly; just moving with it - showing G I like it - I want it.

G's got his hands around my cock, pushing

back and forth, back and forth. I'm writhing with the pleasure, and maybe, just a little pain.

He's cradling my balls, cupped in his hand. He's running his tongue around the base of my glans. Then he's drawing me into his moist mouth, there's a slight sexy, slurping noise. G knows what he's doing.

I'm lying with my eyes closed.

Sometime, Gene stopped sucking on me, he's no longer kneeling on the floor, but now he's astride me; his back is to me. He lifts up his bum and brushes his anus against my stiff dick - pauses for a moment. I open my eyes. I watch as his hairy arse comes toward my face.

So there we are, now 69, his mouth round my dick, and his dick thrusting into my mouth. Gene's on top. He's heavy. It hurts me. I try to lift him up by his pelvis, by pushing, like some supine weight lifter, but I ain't no Charles Atlas.

"No Gene, no. It hurts!"

I turn on my side. Me and G side by side. Sucking each other. Gone - Gone. The blood pumping. G's groaning - gasping - sucking - thrusting. I'm holding his dick in my hand, using loads of saliva to keep him lubricated. His dick is glistening, sticky - wet with saliva, semen. He's making forceful thrusts with his groin - faster, harder - I like it - he's not thinking about me.

I'm concentrating on pulling it off. Next thing I know is Gene's pulled away - abruptly he's pulled his dick out of my gob and he's turned around, so he's facing the same way as me - we're facing each other now. He's kissing me deep; it's all saliva and each other's semen, and strong, hard, sexy - his hand around the back of my neck, holding, pulling, tight.

Somewhere along the line G's got his fingers in my mouth, pushing, sliding, probing. It all feels a bit weird. Then he's slipping his dripping fingers down between my thighs - round my penis, scrotum, dripping, wet. Then his fingers are prodding at my anus. He's got both hands down now. I'm on my back. He's pushing my knees up around my face. Now he's kneeling on the bed. He's cupping my balls with one hand, and trying to shove his dick in my arse with the other.

"Stop," I say, "Stop."

G doesn't want to stop. I don't like it.

"Get a condom," I say.

What the fuck is going on?

I dunno. I've never had anal sex, and if I'm gonna have it, I want to make my own decisions, how, with who, when.

"I don't have any fucking condoms. Where are yours?" demands Gene.

"I don't have any," I lie.

"Fuck. Fuck," says Gene.

Funny how things change. One minute I want it, then I don't. One minute Gene's all lovely, gentle, sexy, then he's not.

Now he's angry. I'm angry. I feel like a girl. I want to make my own decisions. And after all the blood pumping and testosterone, pheromone, etc., etc., we're stood there; angry, our hard-ons soft; even the drugs are wearing off.

Gene picks up his clothes.

I say, "What are you doing?"

He doesn't answer. He goes into the living room. There's a couch in there. I hear the rustle of foil, the *click*, *click*, of his lighter. I climb into my bed. It's cold. I pull the duvet up around my chin and curl into the foetal position.

Twenty·four

I wake to the bang of the front door. I feel groggy. I get up and rush out into the corridor. I open my front door, quickly - the icy wind snaps around me, around my bare shoulders, my naked genitals. These flats have communal walkways in the front. I stand out - lean over the wall, so I can look down into the quadrangle below. Yeah, there's G.

It's weird watching someone you know, at a distance. Think about it - you know it doesn't actually happen that often in life. People don't like being watched like that - they get all self conscious.

G's about to go out through the entranceway, disappear from my view, when he raises his hand, up above his shoulder, hand up, fingers tight together. Then he spreads the fingers slightly, and without turning around, he waves. There is nobody else in the courtyard. I look around. Gene's gone.

I'm staring out at a crisp, dark, early morning. I'm looking at my own surroundings - it's all familiar, but very unfamiliar - lost inside myself. It's freezing cold. I turn, when I hear a door opening down the landing. My next door neighbour appears in her sari, with her little boy and the baby girl. She's horrified. She clutches the baby to her bosom, wraps her hand around the little boy's head and draws him back into the flat, gibbering away in Bengali. The look on her face! I smile. I shrug. I walk back into my flat - run a bath - get ready for work.

"Fuck it."

Twenty·five

A gig. A *real* gig. Somehow Gene had negotiated with organisers of The Soho Jazz Festival a support slot in The French House, Frith Street.

The upstairs room was by no means large - it looked bigger than it actually was due to the fact that one wall was covered by mirrors. At a guess I considered it could only hold fifty people, but it was packed. The audience was lively, a mixture of old Sohoites and young cool beats. I was excited. The audience were there for the jazz, but it was up to me and G to show them poetry was gonna be the new rock 'n' roll. I was nervous - Gene had still not arrived. Our rehearsals had got less and less and it seemed G's time was being taken up more and more by Maria. Where is he? He knows how important this is.

I had introduced myself to the MC; some fat old jazzer in a very loud purple and green check suit. Now he was agitatedly telling me we should have been on ten minutes ago. I tried to placate him. "Give us five more minutes, my partner will be here any moment."

"Five minutes, and if he doesn't turn up, you're out," he states, matter-of-factly.

I was panicking. It was looking like Gene had really blown our chances.

Someone clasped my hand, "Darling, oh how lovely, so *you're* the poets." I turned to face a middle-aged, red-haired woman, dressed in a multi-coloured gypsy dress and a black, crocheted spider-web shawl. She wore deep red lipstick, which ludicrously clashed with her pancake powdered face.

"It's so good that they've brought back poetry to Soho." Her grip tightened on my hand, as she stared into my eyes.

"You're too young to remember, but I know you'll understand - in the fifties this area was Bohemia.... Painters, photographers, writers..... Darling, it was **paradise!**"

She moved closer. As the ruby red lips engulfed me, she breathed red wine and nicotine into my face. All this time my eyes had been darting towards the door. *Where is Gene?*

I hear a familiar laugh coming up the stairs.

Extricating myself from the dreamy-eyed old dear with a "Yeah, yeah, I'm sure..."

I move quickly towards the doorway. Looking down I see Gene with Maria at his side.

"Where the fuck have you been?" I yell down at them.

"Hi Spike."

"I said, where the ***fuck*** have you been?"

Gene was now with me at the top of the stairs.

"Chill out Spike, I'm here. When are we on?"

"Come on!" I turned my back to him and angrily walk to the microphone. I turn. Scowl at Gene. He removes his long black coat - bundles it to Maria. People have stopped their conversations, and are all facing me. I simmer with rage waiting for Gene to join me. Gene comes towards me with a stupid smirk. I shout into the microphone, "We are The Big City Beats."

Gene arrives and without so much as a glance begins the opening lines of 'Mortality'. The poem progresses. I await my cue where Gene's supposed to say "Everything is **death**." He doesn't! The bastard! He's missed it out altogether, and then... and then he's just stood there - looking at me - *as if it was* ***my*** *fault.* I rescued us by launching into 'War Of The Words'. It was a bad start.

We soldiered on.

The high spot of the set is where I pull the gun. Fuck! Suddenly I realise *I do not have the gun!* Where is it? Oh no, I've left it in the drawer of my bedside cabinet. Fuck! I catch Gene's eye, and mouth the words "The gun." Gene shrugs as if he doesn't care. Perhaps he doesn't understand! I move closer and whisper in his ear, "I haven't got the gun!"

Gene mutters out of the side of his mouth, "It doesn't matter."

What? What's going on?

Maybe we can improvise, maybe Gene's got some plan that can save us. And then...

The old pancaked dippy gypsy woman is booing; waving her cigarette holder and wine glass around – booing. She's turning her head towards the audience, trying to get everyone else to join in, "Booh, booh."

And then...

Gene says...

"Thanks, that's it. Goodnight."

WHAT?

I was furious. We walked through the crowd back towards Maria, waiting by the bar.

"That was fucking terrible," I spat.

Gene replied, "Spike, it doesn't matter."

I couldn't fucking believe what I was hearing. I needed some distance and went to the other end of the bar and ordered a double whiskey.

I stood and drank - the jazz band came on. I watched. The trumpeter began blowing a soulful rendition of the Miles Davis classic A *Kind Of Blue*. I ordered another whiskey.

Eventually Gene came over to my side of the bar and offered to buy me a drink. I was waiting for Gene to say some words of apology - but nothing. He smiled as he handed me the whiskey, then he turned towards an old man in an expensive suit. Gene's gestures would indicate that he knew this man quite well.

The tempo of the music was increasing and the audience were responding as the band played be-bop. I watched, but out of the corner of my eye I kept noticing Gene in an animated conversation with the rich stranger. Then I overheard Gene mention the tour. My ears pricked up. In amongst the din I heard Gene say, "A boy and girl routine will be a lot better - more marketable."

The old guy was nodding in agreement - then his eyes met mine - briefly - he furtively looked away. I was intrigued and then shocked, when Gene went on... "Don't worry about Spike, I'll sort it out. He can't cut it these days anyway."

It was like a hammer blow. I stood transfixed - stunned. I gripped the bar rail.

I couldn't look at Gene. I grabbed my coat - pushed my way passed Maria - down the stairs and into the Soho night.

Twenty-six

Over the next few days I couldn't get hold of Gene. I tried and tried to contact him. I asked in all his drinking haunts: The Lord Rodney's Head, Murphy's, The Three Cranes. Nobody would tell me anything. It's as if he'd disappeared. The bastard! What about us?

Twenty-seven

Then things got weird in E1.

I stand, looking into the courtyard of the Grove, and consider my options. Rhys? No, he's fucking mad. Gareth? No, he'll be at work. Nigel! Yeah, Nigel sees Gene a lot.

I cross the pot-holed, litter-strewn courtyard and enter the dark corridor in which Nigel's flat is located. Nigel's door had a sign in the glass that said, 'Enter the age of destruction'. I knocked.

"Come in," a voice called out, "there's nothing to steal."

Maybe this was supposed to be flippant or funny. My own front door had three mortise and one yale lock - I don't think I was particularly paranoid - just the reality of living in the East End.

"Nigel, where are you?"

The tiny entrance-way was dim, all the Grove flats were dim, but it seemed particularly dingy, and there was a decaying smell.

"Spike, is that you?"

The voice emanated from the bedroom.

"You OK?"

I put my head round the door and into the gloom. Nigel was in bed, fully clothed, smoking a roll-up cigarette.

"What's this, trying to keep down the heating bills?"

"No, I'm sick - flu."

I knew it was the come down off smack.

"Kicking a small monkey off your back?" I said.

Nigel shrugged. "Have you seen Gene?"

I was going to ask the same question.

"No," I replied, "I was going to ask the same question."

"Aw."

"What's going on?" I said.

"I'm sick Spike. Gene's disappeared?"

"Looks like Nigel - he didn't tell me anything."

"Me neither."

This is strained, to say the least. Nigel has sunk into lethargy. He looks OK, but he's not really with it. He's thinking about something else.

I go to make tea.

"It's a mess," Nigel warns.

He's right. Nigel is usually so meticulous about his home - meticulous nearly to the point of obsession. I survey the disorder. The sink, which is the only place to wash (as there are no bathrooms), is stacked high with dirty dishes. The bin needs emptying. Empty take-away cartons, chocolate bar wrappers, general junk food detritus litter the kitchen top. The carton of milk, stood on the draining board, is curdled.

"There's no milk."

"No. I'm broke Spike."

Our conversation is stilted. The flat has a sad, unhealthy vibe. It's funny what people's feelings can do to confined spaces. It's a ground floor flat - bad light - dark, dingy, oppressive and it smells of things dying, decomposing... I don't want to be here.

"I'll go get some milk," I offer reluctantly.

"It doesn't matter Spike"... (awkward pause)... "Spike?"

There is an awkward pause. I begrudgingly respond and enter the gloomy bedroom.

"I'm sick - I'm broke - I need to get away." Nigel's eyes are begging. He looks sad - scared - pathetic.

"Yeah?" I say, to myself more than to Nigel, "We all need to get away."

Nigel isn't interested in my cynical musings, he's a desperate man. He begins to cry. I feel trapped.

"I need a break Spike. Get away. Get better."

I'm stood there, wishing I wasn't.

"It's OK Nigel. You're OK. You'll get better."

Nigel's blubbering proper now.

"I've been depressed. Really depressed. I'm a failure. I'm a coward. I've been thinking of suicide. I may as well. Nobody would miss me. "

This is terrible. Why me God? Why me? I have an overwhelming desire to slap Nigel hard across his pathetic blubbery face. I feel like I'm being conned. Suicide talk is such a strong lever in the emotional blackmail toolbox. I try acting human, concerned.

"Don't talk like that Nigel, everyone would miss you..." I couldn't actually think who everyone was.... "I'd miss you." I hate myself. Why do I keep ending up in situations I do not know how to control? Nigel stops gasping and crying for a moment. The bastard knows he's got me.

"Look Spike, I'll level with you, I've been thinking of going to Australia."

"Australia. Who do you know in Australia?"

"I know someone - I've been writing to them - in Sydney." Nigel is being ridiculously melodramatic. It's sickening.

"Yeah?" I venture.

Nigel hangs his head, and begins noisily sucking in air, then making this ridiculous groaning noise. I can tell he's going to start sobbing again. I move closer to the bed. I reach out, put my hand on his shoulder.

Nigel suddenly grabs my outstretched hand with his clammy wet fingers. I want to recoil. I didn't.

"Yes!" cries Nigel. He looks up at me all tear-stained face, all earnest, pleading... "Spike, I'm gay."

I let him hold my hand. I calmly say, "Nigel, I don't care if you're gay." I didn't. I suddenly didn't care at all about Nigel and his pathetic little life. It actually flitted across my mind that if I had Gene's gun, I'd shoot this poor, sad fucker - put him out of his misery.

Nigel is starting to blub again. He is being so ridiculously melodramatic. He's getting all camp and affected. He begins to giggle.

"Yes, I'm an old queen, always have been luvvie."

I don't know what response he expects but I am reviled. I pull my hand from his grasp. He's giggling, all slimy and obsequious. I would dearly love to punch him till I heard bone break - mine or his. I hate him. I hate myself. I hate - most of all I hate Gene.

"Stop it Nigel - stop it!"

I bring my open hand hard down onto his pathetic face. He lets out a repellent, piercing scream, and backs away, pulling his knees up to his chin - his face is all bloody, distorted, ugly. I want to bash him, smash him. He's wriggling and squealing, like some scummy disgusting animal. I raise my arm up. I wish I had a club.

Nigel is huddled in a ball. He's wailing. Then I suddenly get a huge insight into what is actually taking place. This is what he wants. The sad masochistic, disgusting pervert, wants me to hit him, hurt him, even kill him. I'm raging. I kick the bed with my full force; it judders. Nigel makes some pitiable sobby groan type noises, biting onto the sheet.

"Fuck you!" I bellow at the top of my lungs, **"FUCK YOU!"**

I turn. Stand there. The blood and adrenaline is pumping through my temples. I feel disorientated, confused. I want some daylight, some clean air. I reach into my inside jacket pocket, take out my wallet and remove a twenty pound note. I catch Nigel's eyes staring up at me from the bloodied pillow, wide, expectant. This is sad. Life is sad.

My life is heavy with sadness and loss and emptiness. I could cry into the vast shadowy chasm that seems to be all around me - within me. My voice softens - suddenly a huge wave of calm has descended on me.

"Here Nigel, here's a twenty, it's all I've got."

Nigel scrabbles for the note, "Aw thanks Spike, thanks."

"Er, I'm sorry Nigel."

"Yes Spike, yes, it's alright. I need to get away, go to Australia. I will. This'll help - honestly."

I hated smack. I hated what it was doing to people - people I knew. Fucking smack. What's happening these days? Fucking smack heads - they're lost. You can't trust them. They lie. It's sad, but they even lie to themselves. I dunno. Maybe Nigel truly believes he's going to Australia, but I know with all his stupid posturing, and good intentions, I know my £20 is gonna get him out of bed and round his dealer's, and then... yeah, he'll go on vacation... in his head. He won't even need to leave the couch, with his chin on his chest in a hypnogogic gouch he'll go on vacation to Australia, on Zargon, in the land of Nod.

As I left the flat and moved down the dim corridor towards the courtyard, I could swear I heard Nigel laughing - laughing at me.

There is a grey dusty wind vortexing dryly, around the crumbling, yellow brickwork, mixing the torn scraps of yesterday's faded newspaper with the tattered fragments of my unresolved memories, and London holds no illusions for me anymore. In other places, maybe, daffodils dance in the moist Spring breeze, and the air tingles with the thrilling prospect of summer. I wouldn't know - not anymore. I felt grey and old and grimy. I had no answers - no answers.

Twenty·eight

I do not know what propelled my steps. My thoughts are reduced to some subliminal level; I do not even have any desire for coherence or sense. In my nostrils is the smell; the smell of the East End, a smell of concrete and asbestos, of dogshit and old age. I am stood in front of the security door of G's tower block. I had telephoned many times in the last month - even the answer machine did not respond. Everything is dirty and damaged. There I am, just stood in front of the teak and wired glass division that guards the entrance-lobby. I have to see Gene.

I can see the door of one of the lifts; it opens and a little blond girl in a pink dress comes towards the main entrance. She has a Jack Russell puppy in her arms. I stand there. As she approaches I see she has a severe limp; every step makes her little face contort into a mask of pain and horror. I watch through the wired glass as she props her frame at a crazy distorted angle and pushes down on the handle with her elbow. I accept my cue and pull the hefty door open to let her out. She says nothing. I hold the door and watch as she lurches away, whispering secretive, unintelligible words to her little dog. Everything is quiet and heavy with horror, ugliness and... I enter the foyer. The lift is open, waiting. I walk in and press thirteen. There is a smell of disinfectant and piss.

I wait outside Gene's flat, staring at the badly painted front door, the old aluminium letterbox. I need to see Gene. Things have to be sorted out; practical matters, matters of commitment. I am stood there with my arms by my side, fists clenched, staring at the black plastic numbers. I hear a noise. I'm sure I hear a noise from inside the apartment; a door being closed, a television, footsteps. I fall to my knees and lift the letterbox flap. With my mouth to the opening I shout,

"Gene. Gene. It's me. Let me in. Gene."

Silence.

I put my ear to the slot. I hear nothing, or maybe a slight whimpering. I can't be sure. But of one thing I am sure. I know. I have no option, I have nowhere else left to go. I'm thinking I'll just pound with my fists, my feet - make such a noise that there is no alternative. One more time I shout through the letterbox,

"It's me, open up. Gee-n-n-ne, it's me Spike."

I hear a faint voice, "Spikeez, eez zat yooz?"

Maria!

"Maria, it's me, open up. It's me."

I stare through the letterbox slot. My face pressed against the soiled paint work. There's a nylon hairy draft excluder. I can't see anything!

I hear a shuffling, then the fumbled disengaging of locks, and a muffled stream of muttered, frightened, apologetic Italian. The sliding of bolts. I rise, take a step backward. Finally the door opens, just a little; the security chain is still on. Maria's face is in the gap. I don't know what I must've looked like, but her expression was one of fear, pain.

"Hello," I say, stupidly.

The door closes again. I hear the chain being undone, then there I am. There is Maria; she looked shit. Her dark eyes were watery with black circles around. Her skin seemed grey, waxy, her full lips looked pale, insipid... I'd never seen her without make-up. She's wearing a crumpled cotton night-dress, espadrilles all broken and flattened at the back. She looks small, faded somehow. What is happening? Has my very existence become a voyeur of ugliness? Life wasn't meant to be like this. What is happening? She stands there in the hallway, holding the door.

"I'm sorry," I say, cos I can't think of anything else. I am sorry.

"Eetz OK Spikey, Gene eezent 'ere."

I just walk past her. Maybe I believe Gene is inside - I don't think so - I don't think I believe in anything. I advance along the narrow corridor, past the toilet - the door is open, past the bathroom - the door is open. The bedroom door is closed, I open it and peer in. The mattress is covered only by a base sheet, the sheet is grubby, crumpled, the blinds drawn. No G.

"Spikee - no. Gene, eez not ere."

I pull the door to, walk past the open kitchen and into the living room. The whole place is unkempt, not incredibly messy, just neglected, the smell is there. It's the smell that I encountered at Nigel's. It is the smell of Dying.

The living room is predominated by a huge black leather couch; there is a duvet and pillows crumpled on it. The TV is on, no sound.

"So sorry. I sick, cold. Watch TV, yes? Sorry, I move ziss."

She struggles with the duvet and pillows. I let her. She shuffles down the corridor and into the bedroom. I sit on the leather couch - it is warm. Maria re-enters the lounge. She stands framed in the doorway, looking pathetic, sorrowful, confused.

"Where is he Maria? What is going on?"

She blusters a sentence in pidgin English/Italian, then begins to sob uncontrollably. The tears are pouring down her cheeks. I rise from the couch. She covers her face with one hand, and waves the other about in my direction, saying, "No, no..." I sit back down. She stops sobbing. Do I feel sorry for her? This is all so painful, there is so much pain. I feel like crying. I am confused. My world makes no sense at this moment in time. It is a world with too much suffering, and I want comfort. There is no comfort. No, I don't feel sorry for her, I feel sorry for myself.

"Maria, what is it? What's wrong?"

"Gene, ee zay two weekz. Already Spikee, one month. I sick."

Maria looks so vulnerable, fragile. The night-dress she is wearing has long sleeves and a buttoned up neck, and ends well below the knee, but I know underneath that thin layer of crumpled cotton she is naked.

"Where is Gene? What's he doing? Why are you sick?" I ask, but I know.

Maria is withdrawing from heroin. G must be somewhere scoring. I know, but I do not want to know.

She looks at the floor, then slowly lifts her head, like some poor, naughty child. She looks at my face with her dark, watery eyes. I feel a twinge in my loins. Underneath the sick junky is a potentially voluptuous woman. Gene is away, she is sick.

(I did not tell you this, because on a 'need to know basis', I figured you wouldn't need to know, but when I got home to my flat, after work, that fateful day after G and I had attempted, you know...? Anyway, I was just cleaning up in the living room, emptying the ashtray and stuff... And I was just lifting a cushion, to fluff it up, and there, on the couch was a tiny packet, made out of a piece of glossy magazine. It looks like a tiny envelope - one and a half inches by three quarters. I unwrap it and find it's got a bit of brown powder in it. I know '*the brown*' is heroin. Anyway, I kept it.)

Maria is sick; suffering the effects of heroin withdrawal. I have some heroin. I feel a stirring in my loins, and I remember the booth, the blond wig. I blurt out, “Maria, I have some heroin at home. I could get it for you...”

Her expression changes from sad victim, to wide-eyed expectant victim. I like this.

“Ooh yez Spikee, very much, pleaz.”

I can’t remember ever being in this kind of position before. I feel like a steel shutter has closed across my heart. I don’t care; I calculate. I’m thinking, *“Fucking whore. Fucking junky. I’ve got it - you want it. How much is it worth to you?”*

“I’z ave zee money ere.”

She fumbles in her clutch bag, takes out some notes, and waves what looks like about two hundred pounds. I wasn’t expecting money as payment - not at all. I know to a sick junky whore this has got to be worth something more than money.

“No, no Maria, I don’t want money.“

“No?” she says.

“No,” I say.

Her expression is quizzical, and maybe a little scared. I give full eye contact. I feel we are getting some kind of understanding here.

“Let me go get the stuff, then we’ll talk about payment.”

A harder, tougher expression comes across her face. I think she might say something. She says “OK.”

I turn to leave. Maria says, “How long you be - eh?” Her voice has a more clipped, harder tone.

“An hour.”

“Ere.” She is holding out a twenty pound note. “Take a taxi. Pronto - eh? I make-a zee call.” She picks up the telephone receiver and dials a mini-cab, she speaks in Italian. “Eetz-a downstairs when you come.”

I leave the flat and press the down arrow on

the brushed-steel panel. I wait. Descending in the lift I am thinking about sex and violence and death, and ... they are all as one. I hit bottom. When I open the teak and wired-glass main door, the taxi is outside. The driver is a squat swarthy mutant, with a flat cap & vest. He has thick, curly, black hair all over his neck and shoulders. He smokes a filthy cheroot. I tell him my address.

When we arrive I tell him to wait. Once I've gotten the smack and some condoms from my bedside cabinet, I get back in the stinking car, and tell him to return. He has not said a word. Even when I ask the cost of the fare, he does not reply. He simply takes the proffered twenty and gives me a greasy ten in return.

I ascend.

I knock at the flat door.

I say, "Maria. It's me."

The door opens and there she is, still in her nightie, but she looks different. She doesn't look as pale and puffy. She's put on some make-up. I walk into the living room and sit on the couch. I take the packet out of my wallet, hold it out to her. She stands there, the desire and expectancy shows in every fibre of her being, but she is trying to act cool.

"Here, take it," I say.

She picks the small wrap from my palm.

"I go in zee bathroom, no? I not be long."

"No Maria, you can do it here."

She looks at me quizzically. But I know that whatever she may be thinking about me and the way I'm acting is secondary to her obsession with getting some opiates into her system.

She unfolds the envelope and looks at its contents.

"Its good," she says.

Then she places the open pack carefully on

the glass-topped coffee table. She turns and goes into the bedroom. She comes back with what looks like a little black leather make-up bag. The huge black couch is the only seating in the living room, so she sits next to me, with the leather make-up case on her lap. I watch as she takes each item out and delicately places them on the coffee table. First is a stainless steel teaspoon wrapped in tissue. She unwraps it and I see that the handle has been bent into a crazy ark and the back of the bowl is completely blackened by soot. Next is a clear plastic disposable hypodermic in its cellophane wrapper, then a box of matches, a piece of cotton wool, a greaseproof paper envelope with the same dimensions as the one that contains the smack, and finally what looks like a condom packet; a red and white vacuum sealed foil square with the name 'Sterets' on it. I look on, amazed, but unmoved.

Maria gets up and goes into the kitchen, I hear a cupboard door being opened and closed, then the clinking of a glass, the tap running. She returns with a tumbler half filled with water and one of those squat, night light candles with the aluminium foil base. I sit back with my arms along the sofa back, my foot crossed onto my knee. I try to look blasé - really I am disgusted. My disgust at the life I find myself inhabiting - my disgust at the lives that others inhabit, and mostly my disgust of G, meant that everything was exactly as it should be. I am fearful. I am angry. I try looking nonchalant. I am about to see somebody self inject. I have never seen anybody self inject before - never. It is disturbing - but I look on with a morbid fascination - the same kind of fascination that people have when passing by the aftermath of a car crash. I am morbidly incredulous. I know why I am doing this.

Maria casts a glance towards me as she

picks up the open wrap that contains the heroin. I do not catch her eye, just stare as she lifts the small paper square, and holding the edge over the spoon she taps out the powder. She gently places the spoon onto the table's surface. Then she picks up the hypodermic's packet and tears the cellophane wrapper. She takes out the syringe and removes the needle's plastic guard. Then she dips the needle-tip into the glass. She draws up some water into the hypo's barrel. Then she holds the tip of the hollow needle over the spoon's bowl and squirts a fine train of water into the brown powder.

She places the empty syringe on the table and picks up the second small packet, which she opens and begins tapping some of its off-white powder into the liquid in the spoon.

She takes a matchstick and uses the unsulphered end to gently stir the spoon's contents.

She strikes the same match on the side of the box, and uses it to ignite the tea light. Then she holds the blackened spoon over the candle's flame; moving it gently from side to side, stirring it with the uncharred end of the now spent match.

She tears a piece off the wad of cotton wool and rolls it between her thumb and forefinger into a tiny ball; she drops this ball into the spoon. All the brown liquid in the spoon's bowl is absorbed into the cotton ball.

Maria inserts the tip of the needle into the cotton ball and slowly pulls up the plunger. The barrel fills with a yellowy brown liquid.

She is holding the syringe in her right hand. Her thumb is on the plunger, her middle and index fingers are either side of the barrel's base - the needle tip pointing ceilingward. With the middle finger of her left hand she softly flicks the barrel - twice - three times. Then, just like in those hospital serials, she pushes in the plunger - just a bit - and a tiny jet of liquid squirts upward from the hollow tip of the needle.

She then places the full syringe lightly between her teeth.

I sit, I watch - fascinated. I do not move.

"Geev-a me yor belt - huh."

I'm too preoccupied with trying to act nonchalant to understand - she is talking with a syringe in her mouth.

"Yorz-a belt - yes?" Maria points at my waistband.

"Oh, oh," I say, comprehending, and unbuckle my belt, pull it through the belt-loops and hand it to her.

My mind is racing.

This whole scenario is one of observance to a well worn ritual I do not understand. I have no idea why she has asked me to remove my belt.

Does she know I expect sex for the life-giving gift I have brought her? Yes I think she does.

Is she going to make me pull my pants down? It's too farcical.

Is she intending to whip my buttocks?

Is she trying to humiliate me?

My mind is racing...

But it is none of these things she has on *her* mind...

She slots the tongue of the belt through the buckle and makes a small loop, which she puts her arm through.

Now I understand.

I understand now - she is using my belt as a tourniquet! She pulls the loop tight, just above her bicep. With the finger-tips of her other hand she taps the inside of her elbow to (I presume) make a vein rise. Then she takes the hypo out of her mouth, very carefully aligns it along the risen vein, and suddenly the needle tip has pierced the skin.

I am taken aback.

She glances up at me. I hope I am looking composed. I try to. I'm sure a faint smile flickers over her lips. With her thumb-nail she slightly pushes up the plunger. I see a delicate fern of blood growing inside the liquid.

Everso gently she leaves the full syringe laying on her fore-arm, as she slackens the tourniquet. Then holding the barrel between her fingers, with her thumb she pushes the plunger right down, slowly, steadily - her eyes fixed in concentration.

Then, with the needle still under her flesh, she prizes back the plunger, and draws pure red blood into the barrel. I am shocked. With the syringe half full of her own blood, she again pushes down on the plunger, emptying the barrel.

For a moment she closes her eyes.

Her face softens, she seems so relaxed. And then she opens her eyes and... she looks different; more animated - I dunno - stoned.

She pinches the needle and pulls it out of her vein. A trickle of blood runs down her forearm. She picks up the foil-wrapped, vacuum-sealed 'Steret' pack, and tears it open to reveal a folded wet-wipe, which she uses to remove the trail of blood. Then she places her hand onto her shoulder; the wet-wipe caught in the crux of her arm - she leans back into the couch and closes her eyes.

"Mm-mm," she says, savouring the pleasure that is so obviously infusing her whole body.

I sit. I wait. She is evidently not with me, at this moment. She is somewhere else, and happy. She has got what she wants. I sit. I wait. I look at her, in her cotton nightie. I look at the bulge of her breasts. I look at her bare ankles; there are small black hairs stubbling through. I slide my arm further along the back of the settee, towards her. Then I wrap my arm around her shoulder and pull her towards me. Her eyes open. She says, "Uh," and squirms slightly. She is not compliant, but likewise she is not resistant. I kiss her clumsily on her lips. She is not really responding, but I do not care. She owes me - she knows that much. She was sick - now she is well. I am the man who can keep her well. She does not know that I only had the one bag of gear - she does not know that - she owes me one - she is not stupid.

I turn my body - one knee of one leg on the couch - the foot of the other leg on the floor. With my left hand in-between her shoulder blades and my right hand in the small of her back, I turn her and pull her towards me. So now she is half sitting, half lying on the settee. She is like a rag doll. I throw myself on top of her. I'm kissing her face, her neck. My right hand is pulling at the bottom of her nightie.

"Spikee, no please - I smell."

She did. She smelt of wet dustbins, and her skin tasted musty, salty. I said nothing, just knelt up and unzipped my fly. She turned her head into the couch. I pushed my pants down over my arse, and pulled a condom from my pocket. I tore open the packet in my teeth, and quickly rolled the lubricated latex over my semi-erect dick. She groaned a slight disgusting groan - she knew she owed me this.

I grip her ankle and push her leg up onto the couch. Her body tenses as I put my hand up into her cunt. I slide her nightie up, and there I am, looking at her dark hairy pubes, and the dark stubble on the inside of her thigh. It turns me on. I slide my middle finger into her hole - she flinches. I pull my finger out - there is a smell like dead fish – I'm glad to be wearing a condom. I guide my sheathed member into her stubborn hole and push hard. She shrieks. I scream. It hurts, but I don't stop.

I held her by the wrists and pumped away, till grunting like an animal, I shot my wad. All this time Maria had her head turned away from me, her eyes closed and her face twisted in a grimace of pain. I didn't care.

When I pulled my dick out, the condom was split. My knob was bleeding and sore - painfully throbbing.

"You'd better not have AIDS," I said.

Maria put her feet on the floor, pulled down her nightie and began sobbing - shaking her head. I wanted to hit her.

"Don't worry," I said, "You'll catch nothing off me. I'm clean."

She let out a wailing groan and began crying more, holding her head in her hands. The noise was obscene.

I said, "You're too fucked up to get pregnant, so shut up. Go douche yourself. You'd better not have AIDS."

She was sobbing uncontrollably. She looked disgusting. She got up and went into the bathroom. I heard the door lock. Thank fuck for that. I'd stuffed my dick back into my pants so as not to be humiliated and it was throbbing with pain. I got up and rushed to the kitchen sink. I ran the cold tap, stood on my tip-toes, and pulled my injured dick out of my fly. It was so soothing, splashing my messy knob with the cold running water. It felt better. Then I suddenly panicked about what I'd done, the possibility of infection. The stinking junkie whore had split my dick with her dried-up sandpaper snatch. Fuck!

I took a tumbler off the drainer. Unscrewed the top off the salt cellar. Poured all of its contents into the tumbler, added water, and waggled my poor member in the healing, saline solution. It hurt. It felt good.

Then I heard the bathroom door open. I turned away from the door and zipped up. In my haste I caught my already damaged foreskin in my zipper. **"Aargh. F-uck!!"**

Maria had just gone into the bedroom and I heard the door close. She didn't come to find out why I was screaming.

So I'm on my own, with my poor puckered and damaged foreskin nicked in my zipper. I can't go forward. I don't want to go back. I must. I wrench the tab downward.

"Aargh-ah-ah!"

The pain is excruciating. Maria remains in the bedroom. I'm in fucking agony - but relieved to be free.

I see my foreskin is bleeding big time now. Fuck! I take a massive wadge off of the kitchen roll, run it under the cold tap, and wrap it gently round my poor cock. I push it all back inside my Y-fronts, and immediately see a big damp patch seeping through. Fuck!

I hear the bedroom door open. Maria looks in on me. She's wearing a man's long sleeved checked shirt done up to the neck, a pair of woollen high-waisted trousers, and a pair of brown Dr. Marten shoes. She's got no make-up on, she looks stern, hurt, a bit dykey - Slut - I couldn't give a fuck. Her contemptuous gaze moves down to focus on my pant front. A kind of stern, hurt, but none-the-less haughty, sneering kind of look comes over her stupid face, then she just turns and goes into the living room.

I pull my shirt tails out in a vain attempt to cover the damp patch. My dick is throbbing. I move out of the kitchen, poke my head round the living room doorway. Maria is sat on the couch. The candle is lit. She's tap-tapping the powder into the spoon. She does not acknowledge me. I say nothing, just turn and walk away, down the corridor, towards the front door. I do not try to be discreet. Bitch.

I turn the mortise key, flip the sneck on the yale, and with a loud slam I'm stood out in the corridor - that smell - the smell of communal walkways - of concrete, dirt, linoleum. I walk to the lift and press the down arrow - it lights. I'm staring at the rucked and ruptured corrugated aluminium doors, with the old chewing gum wedged in the grooves and the burn marks where cigarettes have been stubbed. I can hear the rumble of the lift gear. I long to be out of this building. Then I hear Maria's flat door open. She comes out into the corridor - her stupid dykey shoes, trousers, shirt. She's trying to look all tough, but her eyes betray her pleading.

"Spikeez I-a needz more of zis."

She's waving the powder wrap between thumb and forefinger.

The lift arrives. Clunk. The doors open. My head is turned, looking at Maria. My body faces the opening lift doors - I do not want Maria eyeing my damp crotch again with her disdainful expression. I swivel my head back towards the lift - holding in my mind that face - Maria's face at that moment - despair - hatred.

I hear Maria shout, "Spikeez!" Her wailing is overwhelming. But as I step into the open lift, I am more aware of two youths, looking directly at my sodden pant crotch. Fuck.

I hear Maria scream, and run towards the closing lift doors. Everything spins in a crazy frozen moment (and always the smell). One youth says to the other, "Dirty bastard – could've waited," and sniggers to his mate. I glower and feel embarrassed. They snicker and nudge. The lift moves slowly - slowly. I turn my back to them - face the doors. I hear their jibes and comments at my rear. We hit bottom. As the doors are still opening, they both push past me; the last one shoves me backwards. I stumble. He turns and shouts, "Dirty cunt," laughs a jackal laugh, then they both run off, out the back entrance.

I hit my shoulder on the steel wall of the lift, but I do not fall, and I recover quick enough to get out into the entrance-way before the lift doors close again. I run after my assailants, towards a back door, which until now I had never noticed. As I push open the steel and teak door, I am struck by the overwhelming stench of garbage.

I look along the short corridor, and there at the end, silhouetted against the daylight, is the twat that pushed me. He's stood there, bold as brass, leering, taunting "Dirty pissy bastard. Dirty pissy bastard."

I move toward him - when **WHOOMP...** purple - static - warm pain... blackness.

Twenty·nine

The stink of rubbish is in my nostrils, as I wake. There is a pitter-pattering sound. Warm rain is splashing on my face, my shoulders. It's dark. The rotting smell of refuse is overpowering. I open my mouth. This is not rain. It's salty, acrid, it is piss. My head hurts, my crotch hurts, my ribs hurt. I'm being pissed on.

"Gra-ah-ah-blah," I make some kind of protest noise.

"Wha-ah-yee-ow."

I kind of recognise the cat-like end bit of this cry. I lift my head in the gloom.

"What the..."

"Who goes there?" I recognise the dulcet Welsh tones.

"Gareth?"

"Eh?" he retorts.

I get to my knees and push myself up. My left hand squelches into something. My knees, ribs, head, all scream with pain. My eyes are becoming accustomed to the gloom. I'm surrounded by tall Paladin bins. I focus on Gareth. He's obviously pissed. He's pathetically trying to adopt what he must think is some kind of martial Kung Fu stance. It's absurd. I want to laugh, but the pain in my ribs is searing. I scream in agony, "Arh-h-h, I'm..."

"Spike? You scared the fucking daylights out of me."

"Gareth. What the fuck are you doing yer bastard - pissing on me?"

"I didn't know..."

Gareth is actually stood there, in this daft legs akimbo, hands raised Bruce Lee parody, with his knob still out. He's kind of staggering slightly backward. He falls on his arse, hands still raised. Then he begins to laugh. Then he screams a deranged mad scream.

"Spi-i-i-ack".

I'm stood now. It's incredibly painful trying to straighten up. What the fuck is happening? I feel in my jacket pocket for my wallet. It's gone. And my watch - gone. Everything. I think my ribs are cracked. What is happening? Why is Gareth pissing in the Paladin bins at the bottom of G's tower block?

"What you doin' yer Spike, in the bins?"

"I've been mugged. I think my rib's broken."

"Bastards. Where are they - bastards." Gareth looks pathetic sat on his arse - pissed.

"Gar, what are **you** doing here?"

"Oh, oh. I'm round to see if I can see Gene - I heard he's back. I rang the buzzer, there's no reply, so I thought I'd try the back door. Have you seen him?"

"No – no," I say, "Are you sure he's back?"

"Well that cunt Barry in Murphy's said he was back - said he'd scored off him - today."

Gareth was a piss head - why should he be interested in seeing Gene?

"Gar, why do you want to see Gene?"

"Fancied a toot Spike. You know."

I don't know. I'm realising this is part of my problem. I don't know fucking anything. What is going on? Everybody is living their dirty disgusting lives, and taking me for some kind of stupid.

Gareth gets up off his arse. He's got an absurd, pathetic piss-head face - it's almost like those cartoon drunks; eyes like crosses. Fuck knows how he thinks he looks. He's got his drunk, haughty, swaggering demeanour. Twat. Thinks he's better than me. Stupid twat. Thinks he knows something I don't know. Thinks he's better than me - when really he hates himself. All these dumb fuckers, with their lies and deceits make me sick. They're not fooling anyone - except themselves.

Gene's back. Barry says he scored off him today. What does this mean? If he's back, then he hasn't contacted Maria - well not unless he's done it in the time I've been unconscious.

"Gareth, what time is it?"

"Bout ten - later maybe."

I must have been lying in the Paladin bins for hours - five hours maybe.

I take a step. The pain. My ribs are bust. For sure. Gareth's teetering like some spastic automaton. He approaches the back door. Teak and stainless steel - he pulls the handle. There's a creak. It opens.

Everything hurts in me. I've got muck on my hands, in my hair, on my jacket, shirt, trousers - shoes are scuffed. One side of my face is tender and puffy. I've got a splitting headache. I touch my tongue on a molar, the tooth moves slightly in my jaw bone. Ow! The whole lower part of one side of my face is throbbing. I touch my head and feel a matted, sticky mess, and a huge bump. One knee of my jeans is frayed through. My knee is severely grazed. It is a real pain when I attempt to walk. I lift my left leg. Ah. Ah. I'm doubled up, holding my hand on my scalp. When I let my foot back to the floor a jarring pain shoots up from my leg into my ribs.

"Arh-rrgh!"

Gareth turns around - he looks pissed off. He's holding the heavy spring-action door open.

"Comin'?" he says, raising his eyes heavenward.

I would dearly love to smash the fucker's head open.

"Gar - fuck - my fucking ribs - broken - and my leg."

"Fuck off," says Gar," you wouldn't be able to stand if your leg was broken. Come on."

I hate him. I consider groaning and falling over, but Gareth wants to see Gene more than he wants to feign sympathy for me.

He makes a quick move, as if to let the door go. I react with a jerk forward, and again, the flash of searing pain. I'm doubled up cradling my rib cage with one arm and holding onto the wall for support with the other. I lift my head and look into Gareth's eyes with a deep hate, and maybe a bit of patheticness. He just meets my stare with a sneer, then, the twat actually tuts...

"...tuh. If you can't walk - stay here. I'll be quick."

The bastard!

I hold onto the wall and limp forward. I'm seething.

When I get to the door Gareth just lets go and steps inside - which means, again I have to lunge forward. I grab the edge of the door. In that moment the pain is so intense, I cannot even scream. I gasp. Short, childlike intakes of breath, that could be the beginning of a whimper, or sobbing....

The heavy door closes almost completely - my fingers stop it.

"**ARR..RH!**" I scream.

The blow to my fingers overrides all the other aches in my body. My natural reaction would be to pull out my ~~shrieking~~ throbbing hand and stuff it in my mouth; suck the squashed knuckles; stuff the fist into the sanctuary of my moist orifice to constrain the shrieking whimper that is wanting to come forth, but the heavy door clamps it like a vice.

In the silent screaming of this nightmare, I can clearly hear that inside the block, the lift doors are opening. I hear an irritated, “Spi-i-ack! For fuck’s sake!” from Gareth.

“Hold on,” I tersely yell, as loud as I’m able with my bruised lungs that pain every time I try to raise my voice. “Hold on,” I feebly repeat, but immediately I hear the lift doors close.

There is silence. My hand is being squashed. It really hurts.

I hobble my damaged leg closer to the massive door, and grab the handle with my free hand. The effort required causes me excruciating agony - I have to pull with my right hand, which causes my ribs to stab into my lungs. Ah. Ah. I need to take the weight on my right leg - which buckles under the exertion. But the door has released its grip slightly, and I manage to push with my right shoulder and slump my body into the gap. I’m sliding downward with my trunk in the opening. The heavy door closes on my ribs. I c-ca-ca-ca, in little gasps - I want to cry.

I manage to push with my good leg and bad shoulder, and hold the door open long enough to end up with all of me inside. I hear the lock mechanism click into place, a satisfied clunking click. I want to sit down - rest, but there is a puddle of piss immediately inside the door - and fag butts and filth - and in the middle of the piss puddle is a spiral of turd, which has been trodden-in, and walked down the corridor (there’s no point in looking for the sympathy vote in E1).

I limp - bent double - down the shit-smelling corridor, and into the entranceway. I’m stood in front of the lift. The smell of excrement is incredibly overpowering. I look down, and see, whoever the shit-victim was, has scraped a big wadge of turd onto a lolly stick and dropped it by the corrugated aluminium doors. I feel nauseous. I think I'm going to faint.

I press the 'up' arrow on the brushed-steel panel. I hear the lift descending.

I do not understand what is happening. I am here, in the entrance-lobby of Bradmore House, waiting for a lift, waiting to see Gene. I understand that. But also I am not here. Not me. I have a different life, a stabler, slower, safer life, where I go to work five days a week, see my fiancee, maybe go out, have the odd beer with a friend. Right here, right now I am a voyeur on a lifestyle I do not understand. I am a victim, but I will not let them make me a casualty.... The lift door opens. I lurch inside. Shit, piss, disinfectant, stale cigarette smoke. Filth. Fluorescent light. Physical pain. I feel like I'm looking out from inside somebody else's cranium; looking through the eye sockets of somebody else. I feel like I felt when I stuck my face up to the slot in that peep-booth, like when I pushed my face up to G's letterbox. Maria, Maria.

Maria.

Thirteen. Boing. The doors open.

"Sp - Sp - Spike," Gareth is stood there. His face is white. He is gesticulating, pointing down the corridor. He cannot talk properly. He is panicked, pissed, bumbling. I consider slapping him. I make a move. He rushes at me, into the lift, grabs me. He grabs my arm, pulls me. It hurts - really hurts. I smash my fist into the side of his head. He backs off, back into the corridor, looking shocked. If I was not so crippled with pain I would hit him again and again. He stumbles backwards, looking at me with horror, shock. I hope I hurt him. I step out into the corridor. Gareth is wide-eyed with fear. Now would be the time to strike, but every movement is agony for me.

Gareth is watching me. He wants me to say something. Flap about. Panic. I do not want to give him the satisfaction. I am in pain and I feel exhausted. I have had enough. Enough. If only I felt fresher, fitter. If I had a knife or a metal bar.... It is all I can do to stand semi-upright and give Gareth full eye contact. I imagine what Gareth would look like with a screwdriver in his eye. Gareth is stood there blinking, stupidly. For a moment I have a brief flashback and I'm remembering the look on the audience's faces that very first time I pointed the gun. The gun.

Gareth is watching me. He knows he has just looked death in the face. He does not however, know he has just had a reprieve. I would love at least to make him piss himself - something...

Possibly ten seconds (max.) has elapsed.

Gareth waves his hands about some more. Again he tries to speak, "Spike. Keith. Maria ubb-err-ah..."

"Yes," I say, just to shut him up. "Yes."

This is a fucked world, full of fucked people doing fucked things to themselves and to others. I know. I'm one of them.

Holding my rib cage with one arm and holding onto the wall with the other I begin moving towards the flat.

The door is wide open, the lights all on. I stop, I turn. Gareth is still against the wall in the corridor.

"Comin'?" I demand.

Gareth jerks. Like a naughty dog, he coweringly slopes toward me, his eyes on the floor. I revel in the situation, watching him approach, full of fear and dread.

"Gareth!" I hiss.

Head down, he quickens his pace. It goes through my head to wait and give him a slap, but I resist, turn and walk into the flat. I hold the door. Then I hear running footsteps retreating.

"Damn" I say out loud.

I lurch out to see the stairwell glass door banging to. Through the bobbled glass I glimpse the flapping black great coat, then hear the clatter of clumsy feet on the stairs.

"Damn." *Maybe he'll fall and break his neck*, I hope.

I am alone. The corridor has a yellowy, stained fluorescence. It looks like a prison corridor. I am completely alone, and I don't fucking care. I hobble back into G's flat, edging jerkily down the passageway, slowly towards the living room.

There's the couch, the white walls, the mirror. Maria is half lying, half sitting. What's left of her head is at a crazy angle. She almost looks like she's grinning. A lot of flesh is missing from her jaw, and the jaw bone is protruding, a row of bloodied teeth. I look at her. I don't know whether to laugh. I turn and look at the television. The sound is down. It's a programme about jackals.

I pick up the used (and now dry) 'Steret' tissue and push the TV's 'off' button. I wipe around the leather settee, the tissue gets all bloodied. I go into the kitchen. Using the tea towel I wipe the tumbler, the salt cellar, the tap, anything I might have touched. The exertion is painful, but I am determined. I do a thorough job. I move back to the front door, wiping as I go, then finally (still using the tea towel) I pull the front door closed. My thought process is definite, I feel a morbid calm, the like of which I've never known. I don't care what happens. I need to lie down - rest. Everything has stopped in my life for the moment, and that's good.

The corridor is vacant and quiet as I hobble my way through its yellow fluorescent fuzz. I wait for the lift. It arrives empty. I step out into an empty lobby and push the entrance door to find myself in a deserted street. Part of me wishes there was a crowd. I try to walk as erect as I'm able. I wish I was dignified.

Eventually I'm on the Mile End Road. Whitehorse Cabs are on the left. I go into their office. I say I want a cab. Speaking is difficult, and painful. A Maltese guy comes out from the office, and gestures to a red Sierra. I begin walking over. He follows closely. I try not to limp, I try to walk straight. It's impossible. As I near his car, the cab driver does a quick movement and he's abreast of me, in front of me, he opens the back door and kind of offers his hand. I glower, he doesn't know what I'm capable of. He just looks straight at me, expressionless, he turns and gets in to the driver's seat. I get into the back. Bending and then swinging my body down into the seat is agony. I don't care. It feels like soon everything will be ended. I need to sleep.

Thirty

It's impossible for me to remember the following days. I've tried and can't. It isn't important. I can't really say how I felt, not really, but I was resigned to some kind of ultimate conclusion. There hasn't been one. The police came round, about a week afterwards. They asked me questions - when did I last see Gene - stuff like that. They didn't seem particularly interested in me. I answered the best I could. I was surprised that they didn't want more information about G & me - our relationship. It was as if they didn't know how close we were - nobody had told them. Anyway they asked their questions. I answered. They asked me where I'd been that night. I lied to them. I could see they weren't really interested. I thought of feigning inquisitiveness, but couldn't be bothered. I said it was a shame, and both the bobbies nodded in agreement.

That was that. They said if I should hear anything about G I should let them know. I said I would.

When they left I began weeping. I felt unimportant. It's as if I didn't feature - didn't matter. Maybe we weren't close at all. I dunno. How close were we?

Thirty-one

Clare gave me the engagement ring back. She tried to have some kind of row - she said stuff, like she wasn't sure of my commitment any more - where we were going - what was going to happen in the future. I was glad. I couldn't tell her anything. I didn't know anything.

Thirty-two

Time passed, I carried on living. My heart wasn't really in it. I met Anne. She became pregnant. I moved in with her. Anne doesn't demand much of me. It's just as well. I've got nothing to give. Jasmine, my daughter was born, she's two now. I'm glad I didn't have a boy.

Thirty-three

The emptiness is overwhelming.
My life has no substance any more.
Nothing feels real.

E1 is populated by ghosts - that's all they can be. Every time I walk down Sidney Street, I expect to see the twenty-two storey tower block that was Gelston Point; I lived in that high-rise for three years - it isn't there any more.

Sometimes when I'm coming home from work, for no obvious reason I find myself getting off at Whitechapel - I know this place - know it so well - I recognise the smell. But it has changed - I think. It's unreal, like a feeling of déjà vu. I take the steps of a zombie out onto The Strip, turn left; past the Lord Rodney's, The Blind Beggar, Murphy's, The Three Cranes, Passage To India. I don't know anyone. I am never acknowledged by anyone. I keep expecting to bump into Andy & Rhiannon, or Nigel, or Rhys, Gareth - somebody. Sometimes I feel their presence, behind me, but I turn and there's nobody there. I think I may have seen some of these people - occasionally - at a distance - across a crowded bar or in the window of a passing tube train...

Sometimes I'll see someone with bobbed hair and I'll think about Maria... I don't want to think anymore...

I don't know who I am.

Maybe it is me who is a ghost.

I have a letter at home - it's all I have. It arrived, about seven months after... It came from Argentina. Gene said he thinks about me, and that he won't be home again. He included a poem, called 'Distance', its melancholia haunts me...

DISTANCE

I've been here
For quite some time.
Actually
I've been here
For only nine months;
Less.

But I've been thinking.
You do a lot of thinking
When you're away.

Distance.

In time,
Space,
Thought,
Physical being...

Distance.
Time is a great healer,
But it doesn't hide the scars.

Scar tissue heals.
Memory fades.
But really...
It's only...
... Distance.

Why do people climb mountains?
Because they're there.
So much organisation,

So many factors
To consider,
To eliminate
The fall
From top
To bottom...
...The Distance.

How many lovers?
How many friends
Have I known?
Where are they now?

Distance.

Yes
There's a distance
Between you and me,
As you stay
Over there,
And I Try
To make some sense.
But you can't see ...
I can't believe ...
That it's all been a trick,
A joke that's been played on us ...
Which has ended up as ...
Just another length to ...
The Distance.

And the pain
And the suffering?
And the loss?

Will not be in vain.
One day it
Will all just seem ...
One day it
Will all just be seen ...
As another measure of...
...Distance

Distance
...In geography
History
Physics.
Lessons to be learnt...
...Distance.

If I reach out
Far enough
Will I touch
Someone's hand?
Will I touch you?
Or will you be gone,
Or going ...
Fading...
Into...
...
...The Distance?

I didn't tell anyone about the letter. I didn't tell the police - anyone. All that business distresses me. It affected everybody - they all just disappeared.I'm spending my time carrying on with my life. I'm trying not to think too much - it's too confusing. Everything revolves in my mind and gets all convoluted. Memory - it's not a definite thing - it changes. Fact blurs into fiction. Nothing is certain.

Thirty-four

It's ten years since everything happened.

I'm stood on The Strip again. I've just been in The Rodney's - I don't know anybody. There's now a 24 hour store next door - I can't remember what it used to be. It starts to rain. There's a puddle of blood on the pavement. I stare at it. I don't know anything. I don't care what the future holds. I am unsure of the past. I am stood on The Strip in the pouring rain, staring as the pool of blood is spattered and scattered by the dirty raindrops, and rivulets of red find their way to the gutter... to be washed down the drain, into the sewer, to mingle and dilute as it flows into the Thames, around the Isle of Dogs, through the barrier, to Tilbury and in to the North Sea? I don't know. The truth is, I don't fucking know. I am thinking nothing. I stand here, in my skin, trying to remember the role I played - trying to remember. Still looking... still searching... for the Big City Beats.